Battling the Hydra

And other adventures

With (mostly) wild animals

By

Gary Every

Gary Every

ISBN 978 – 1468120103

Dedication

To my niece Delaney "Lemony" Every, who on a beautiful sunshine day while we feeding popcorn to the ducks at a local city park, asked me "Uncle Gary" what are your favorite times seeing wild animals?"

I hope this book answers your question

Gary Every

Battling the Hydra

Introduction

The Naming of Mt. Lemmon

You know which one is Mt. Lemmon right Delaney? It is the tallest mountain in the Santa Catalinas, the mountains which hover over Tucson, Arizona, the town where you live and go to school. The Santa Catalina Mountains were named by Father Kino the ubiquitous exploring friar of the 1700s. Father Kino wrote in his journals that he camped at a place called Santa Catalina de *Cuitabagu*. *Cuitabagu* was an Apache word which meant spring where the mesquite beans grow. The Tohonno O'odham have a long history of living in the shadows of these mountains they call *Babad Duag* or Frog Mountains. The O'odham named the mountains after the canyon tree frogs who adorn the granite canyons filled with waterfalls and deep pools. Anybody who has gone swimming in the deep pools can attest to the wonderful camouflage the gray color of the tree frogs provides as they blend in so well with the rocks and boulders that one frequently does not notice the canyon tree frogs until one almost sits on them and they jump. It is almost as if the rocks are spawning frogs.

Most people refer to the entire mountain range by the name of the highest peak, Mt. Lemmon but many do not know how it got that name. John Lemmon was a Civil War veteran who had survived the horrors of Andersonville Prison. Sarah Jane Plummer wed John Lemmon, and the two of them arrived in Arizona on a "botanical wedding trip" hoping to name some new species in the spirit of exploration. As the newlyweds and their guide, began what they thought was the first ascent of the mountain, the excited husband stopped suddenly at what is now called Dan's Saddle.

Lemmon grabbed a pine tree branch and shouted out "All hats off!".

He had just discovered a new plant species, the "Pinus Arizonica". A little further up the trail they would name a new species of squirrel but later it would turn out not to be a new species after all. Once they had reached the top of the highest peak in the Santa Catalinas, believing they were the first to climb the mountain, their guide carved their initials into a tall tree to signify their feat. They soon found burro tracks which led to a small hunters cabin. The two half starved trappers said there had been others on top of the mountain before them. The men looked around and decided that surely Sarah was the first woman to climb the mountain peak, something which may or may not be true, but irregardless Mt. Lemmon is named after Sarah Jane Plummer Lemmon. For over a century, Mt. Lemmon was the only mountain in the world named after a female explorer. East of Wilcox two round mounds are listed on the maps as the Mae West Peaks but they may wear that name for a different reason. In the 1980's, another female explorer was honored with a mountain peak label when the government of Kenya named a mountain after Jane Goodall.

Delaney when we went to feed the ducks and turtles at Agua Caliente Park you asked me what were my favorite moments viewing wild animals. I don't believe you had any idea what a big question that was. So I wrote this book for you. I hope you like it. I have been blessed to lead a life filled with exploration and adventure. I see that you have a

Gary Every

special spark inside Delaney, and I hope that you find a way
to harness all that extra energy in a way that fills your life
with exploration and wonder. If you do then maybe
someday they will name a mountain peak after you.

Mt. Denali

What is the biggest mountain in the world?

Depends on how you measure it.

Mt. Everest is the tallest mountain in the world, reaching an elevation attained nowhere else but Everest starts way high in the sky and is not actually that big of a mountain. For example Mt. Lemmon in the Santa Catalinas is actually bigger from top to bottom. The biggest mountain in the world from base to summit is Mt. McKinley in Alaska or Denali as it is known to the Native Americans.

Of course Denali is considered the highest mountain in the world only because we humans have a sea level bias. From the bottom of the ocean to its volcanic top, Hawaii is actually the biggest mountain in the world.

Or is it?

Again depends on how you measure it. Who says mountains have to go up? In the heart of the Pacific Ocean the Marinas Trench is big enough to swallow Everest, Denali, Hawaii, and still have room for some of the Andes. So the Marinas Trench is the biggest mountain in the world However I have never been to the Marinas Trench or Hawaii (or Everest) so this is a story about Denali.

There is a bus that rolls through Denali National Park and then drops you off wherever your permit says you can hike. Ranger Roy and I got off the bus and were dropped off on a small hill beside a dirt road. First thing I saw was a grizzly bear on the next hill about a half mile away. Not a regular bear but a grizzly! I have probably seen about fifty black bears during my life but this is the only grizzly I have ever seen in the wild. Luckily it did not come any closer.

We started to hike in a soft rain. I was to learn that it rains almost every day in Alaska, it rains at least a little and some days it rains a lot. You get used to it but the problem with the rain this day was that the clouds covered all the magnificent mountains including Denali, which might be the biggest mountain in the world (depending on how you measure it). The other problem was that I had discovered a shortcut on the map, it took us right through an area called "marsh". A marsh in Arizona is no big deal, it means that the ground is a little soggy. In Alaska it meant the water was about eight feet deep and the only way we could travel was to leap with full back pack from bush to bush grabbing at the branches and standing on the trunk. The bushes were covered with thorns. It was one of the most bloody, cold wet and miserable hikes I have ever been on and then I looked down and realized that the thorny bushes held wild roses. We were traveling through a thicket of wild roses, thousands and tens of thousands of little rust red roses spreading outward in every direction for miles.

The next morning I woke up to a crisp new day without a cloud in the sky so I could see all the magnificent mountains except for Denali which wore a single giant cloud, the only cloud in the entire sky like a lumpy shroud. You could see everything except Denali and you couldn't see Denali at all. At least we were out of the marsh and hiked on dry ground. That night we set up camp on a bluff above a river.

I awoke the morning of the third day and there was a herd of caribou grazing along the river. There were about sixty caribou just below the bluff. I love caribou, both the males and females wear horns. Plus they are so warm and fuzzy looking that if the muppets made deer they would look just like caribou. Then I turned around and there, snow covered white and glistening, was Denali in all her glory. Wow! I knew from the moment I saw Denali that my heart would beat a little faster forevermore and my soul was just a tad bit bigger.

I raised both arms above my head and shouted in exultation. From the river a lonely bachelor caribou answered, tilting back his head and bugling. I stood there and stared at magnificent Denali and could have stared forever but alas, eventually, I needed to journey back to civilization. Now decades later visions of the magnificence of Denali pop into my mind at unexpected moments and remind me to keep my soul large even amidst the drudgery of day to day modern existence. Sometimes I wonder if on beautiful sunny days along a riverbank in Alaska, there isn't still a lovesick caribou who tilts back his head and calls my name into the wind. Al least I hope there is.

Gary Every

Mountain Lion Sunrises

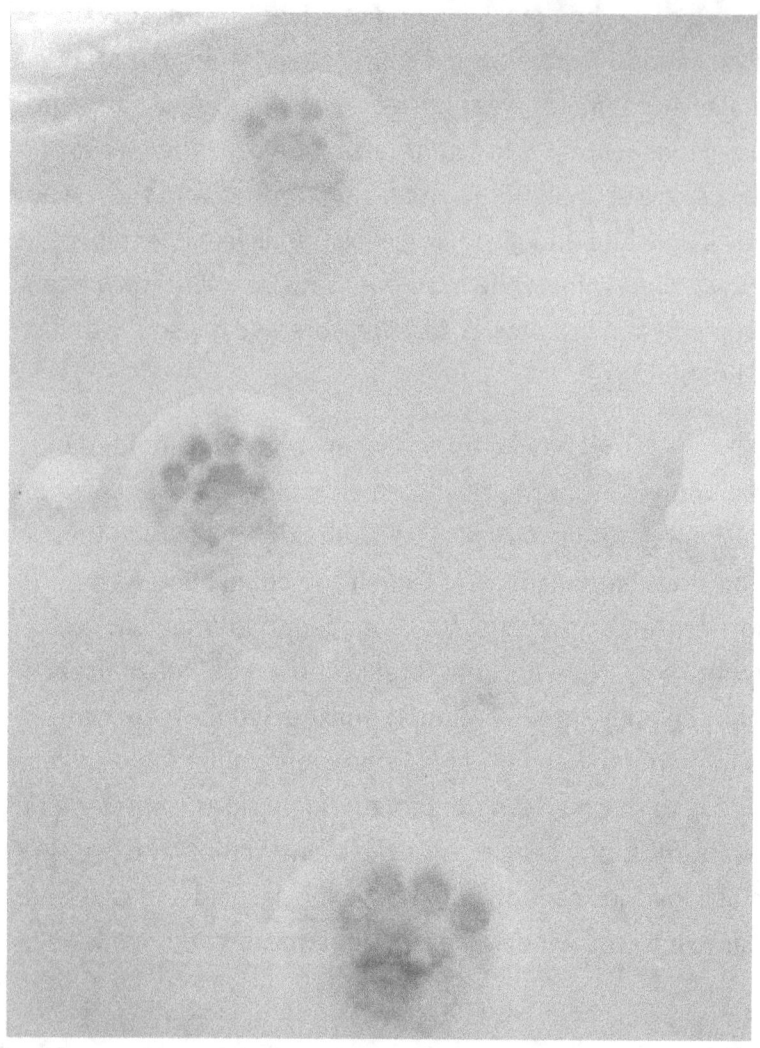

I have only seen three mountain lions in my entire life. Every time I have seen one it has been at sunrise. Every time it has been startling. My favorite was when I was mountain biking in Sedona, rounded a corner and there was a mountain lion. She was huge, female mountain lions are much bigger than males, a hundred and fifty pounds easy. She crouched in the road and glared at me. It was quite a

fierce glare and stopped me dead in my tracks. I didn't
know what to do and was hoping she wouldn't eat me. I
realized it was up to her and not me. We just stood there
and stared at each other briefly. Then the cat took a couple
steps and leapt off the road, over a hill and above the
manzanita bushes on top of the hill. Those massive muscles
rolled beneath the feline fur and that cat leapt thirty feet

across and twenty feet in the air. Then from the middle of
the manzanita thicket the mountain lion leapt again. All I
could see was powerful shoulders, cougar butt, and that
long black tipped tail flying through the air. For just a
second I started to get off my bike and unslung my pack to

retrieve my camera so I could chase that mountain lion and get a good picture. Then I realized I was stupid.

So I stayed on my bike and pedaled away. Native Americans believe that sighting a mountain lion signals change and transformation. Many Native American cultures also believe that the spiritual world is layered atop this world, a veil slips, a window opens and we get a peek at something mysterious and magical. This is why mountain lions only appear at sunrise when the walls between worlds are at their weakest, shimmering softly, giving a hunting mountain lion a brief opportunity to step through to another dimension, where she bumps into my world, where we meet unexpectedly for the briefest of moments. Then the mountain lion disappears back into a world I am mostly unaware of, lapping softly from a secluded mountain pool whose shade I will never know. I am left alone, my heart beating faster, my senses tingling with excitement, knowing I have been transformed and eager to step back into my life and discover how I have changed, in a world just after sunrise when the possibilities seem infinite.

Big Sur Zebras

So there I was driving along California Highway 1, following the Pacific Coast and rolling through Big Sur. This is one of the most scenic highways in the world with mountains, redwood trees, gulls, comorants, cranes, egrets, seals, sea lions, and elephant seals. The seals and the birds are cool but the star of the show is the rocky shore line with the waves crashing in the surf, the constant motion of the ocean bashing against the rocks with great sprays of foam and spray. Just south of San Francisco, this is one of the most beautiful stretches of coastal highway in the world so I was surprised when there was a crowd of people and they were all standing on the other side of the road, looking away from the ocean. What could they possibly be looking at?

It was a herd of zebras! It was the damndest thing, there in the middle of California amidst these rolling grassy hills there was a herd of about forty zebras. Zebras grazing, galloping, and cavorting all black and white stripey and stuff. They were beautiful.

Gary Every

Big Sur Zebras

Driving along Highway One, asphalt rolling by,
geometry screaming directions at me,
dotted lines, double yellow lines, right turn only,
stop signs, yield signs, red light, green light, and speed limits
designed to keep our traffic moving in an orderly systematic
fashion
While off to my right,
the ocean...

the beautiful, beautiful ocean,
a world in constant motion
with wave after wave,
tides rolling in, tides rolling out,
flocks of seagulls flying this way and that,
comorants leaping off the cliff,
sea lions floating in the surf,
while flotsam and jetsam from all over the world
washes up on the shore.

So I was surprised when there was a crowd of people
on the opposite side of the road,
staring and taking pictures of something else besides the
sea...
a herd of zebras!
ZEBRAS in California!
Zebras galloping this way and that,
black and white stripes racing through the meadow,
grass waving gently in the ocean breeze.
The zebras are blissfully at home
while totally completely unaware
of being incongruously out of place.
The zebras gallop back and forth
black and white stripes making a mockery
of our system of rules and regulations,
highways, government, and commerce

Battling the Hydra

while the waves laugh and laugh
and the surf crashes on the sand
making some strange gurgling sounds
I can't quite comprehend.

Gary Every

Save The Amaragosa Toad

Ribbitt!

One might expect the Amaragosa Toad to be endangered and indeed it is. For one thing the name is confusing. The Amaragosa Toad is really a species of frog. Another problem is habitat. Being an amphibian that requires, water, marsh and shade in Nevada on the edge of Death Valley means habitat is rare and precarious. In the high desert plains there stands the multi story ruins of the ghost town of Rhyolite. During the height of its gold boom in 1906, Rhyolite boasted a public swimming pool whose water was changed daily in a wasteful display of perceived wealth and luxury. No one lives in Rhyolite today except for a handfull of wild burros and the ghosts. The swimming pool is empty and the ruins vanished.

The water for the swimming pool was pumped from Indian Springs a few miles away. The small clump of trees which comprise Indian Springs stands out for miles in this dry sparse landscape. This small crystal clear pond, the largest source of water for mountain ranges around has been fenced off to prevent public use. It is an attempt to rescue the precarious habitat of the Amaragosa Toad. People are not the problem. At least most of us aren't. One person in particular was the problem and that person, planted crawfish in those Death Valley waters. The crawfish prey upon the tadpoles and the already rare Amaragosa Toad becomes even more threatened.

Rhyolite is deserted, a ghost town. The crawfish and the frogs are the only residents of Indian Springs. The tiny town of Beatty on the other end of the valley holds a couple thousand people. Along the highway there is a thriving business, Fran's Star Ranch where a man can purchase a little female companionship. You know those adopt a highway signs, that claim a business or organization is responsible for a keeping a stretch of highway clean. The soiled doves employed at Fran's Star Ranch have accepted the responsibility of preserving the frog's habitat, capturing and removing crawfish from the healing waters of Indian Springs. The girls sigh as they wade, tiny nets in hand. Being a whore is not an easy job, making love to the ugly and repulsive for money, but still a girl can dream that her well worn love is the only love whose kiss can transform a squat and warty amphibian into a handsome prince charming. These sisters in sin spend all Sunday afternoon working together, "Save the Amaragosa toad!" they cry.

Ribbit!

Kayaking

I started kayaking about twelve years ago. Growing up in the desert any kind of flowing water strikes me as incredibly beautiful. What I did not expect was all the wildlife you see kayaking. Apparently kayaks do not threaten animals. You get to see birds, cranes, ducks, hawks, egrets, vultures, and flocks of noisily chattering red winged blackbirds. Once, I was kayaking Lake Roosevelt with my friend Jerry and we saw two deer on the shore. The deer were fascinated and after we had taken photos we paddled on our way. The deer galloped along the shore, raced ahead of us and stood by to watch us paddle by again. Then they galloped ahead, waiting and watching us float by again.

A favorite kayaking experience took place in Puget Sound outside Seattle. The sound is extremely deep and home to the biggest octopi in the world. Because the sound is so deep I was forced to cling close to the shores of the island. On the bottom of the sea I could see starfish. Far away, out in the deep parts of the harbor I could see the black fins of killer whales poking above the waves.

I was just paddling along and enjoying my day when I began to pull alongside this long floating log. Suddenly the log lifted its head and looked at me. It wasn't a log - it was a sea lion! The sea lion seemed almost as long as me and the kayak and there was no doubt who was faster in the ocean. The sea lion gently did the backstroke and floated alongside me for about twenty feet, submerged under the water with a barrel roll, went on to its back again lifted its head and barked at me. Then it went under water and swiftly swam away.

Gary Every

Raven Souls

    I was walking along the Rim Trail on the south side of the Grand Canyon when a raven dropped from the sky. The blackness of the bird looked startling against the vast panorama of brightly colored rock. The raven hovered above the many fingers and towers of red, purple, and pink sandstones. The black black bird looked even more shocking against the pastel blue sky. Even though he stayed exactly in place, there was plenty of motion in the raven's flight, a brisk wind ruffling his feathers, pushing his wing feathers apart and fraying the edges. The raven hovered in place, hanging at about eye level with me. The raven screamed, his caw echoing off the vastness of the Grand Canyon while the wind howled.

    I stopped my journey to return the raven's stare. We were looking each other in the eye only twenty feet apart but I was on solid ground while the raven was hundreds of feet in the air. I was walking along the rim of the Grand Canyon only a few feet from a precipice which dropped hundreds and hundreds of feet. The wind gusted up from the edge of the cliffs and tossed my hair every which way, making it look like the frayed edges of raven wings.

Imagine being Coronado the conquistador, reading pompous Latin phrases to the Indians, kicking ass through Mexico, Arizona, Cibola, Hawikuh, and Quivira - until - you run smack dab into the Grand Canyon, a place so big that the silence presses into your flesh, stopping you dead. The Grand Canyon is so big that to this day there are still places where no human being has ever set foot. There is this once upon a time tale, a modern urban legend about a Japanese bride and groom, petite, happy, smiling, newlyweds who got married at the Grand Canyon, when a sudden gust of wind billowed the brides wedding gown like a balloon or parachute, lifting her out over the railing; out to where the eagles soar. The heroic groom leapt for his love clutching her ankles and then they both fell consummating as soul mates with gravities kiss.

I stare at the raven but he has turned his gaze some place far away, his body jostling in the air as it is buffeted by the wind. I have always had interesting relationships with ravens. When I was a little boy, my next door neighbor Barry had a raven named King. King learned my name and late in the afternoon when he was sometimes bored, which he often was, King would call my name. I would scramble over the wall and approach his aviary. Often I brought King presents and soon learned he liked shiny things most of all.

Gary Every

My neighbor was forced to get rid of King when the black bird got out of his roost and was cruising the skies above neighborhood. The Harris's dachsund was apparently offended by the renegade black bird and began barking incessantly at King. King was not the sort of bird to put up with such insults and swooped down from the sky, his talons gripping the noisy dachsund at the dog collar, lifting him a few inches off the ground and carrying him a short ways before dropping the weiner dog on his backside. Rumors and gossip spread quickly throughout the neighborhood until they made King sound like some sort of terrifying pterodactyl who might swoop down from the sky at any moment in his quest for fresh flesh and thirst for blood. A new home was found for King.

If you hike through raven habitat bring along a mirror. Odds are pretty good the raven will be at least temporarily fascinated by the mirror. Once while I was working a geology job on Bare Mountain outside of Death Valley I took the mirror for my compass and made it flash in the sunlight. I soon had seventeen ravens circling above me, screeching one after another, cacophony echoing off the canyon walls. Often times when I capture the attention of a raven with a mirror the raven will soon appear to be bored and fly a short distance away, but the next time the trail takes me to a hilltop, when I come as close as humans come to the kingdom of the sky, the raven is suddenly just above me and gives a caw. I reward the black bird with another flash of mirror.

Ravens are now ubiquitous in the southwest but once they were rare. Dwight D. Esienhower must be the patron saint of ravens because it is the interstate highway system that is responsible for the boom of the raven population. The interstates left behind asphalt ribbons of trash and road kill which allowed the scavenging black birds to migrate across the region. Ravens in medieval Europe were known to follow marching armies in giant flocks, feasting upon the battlefield carnage afterwards. Ravens are known to follow packs of wolves. When Coronado's army marched through the southwest battling pueblo after pueblo, ravens followed the armor clad conquistadors.

I stand on the rim of the Grand Canyon, eye to eye with a raven perched atop his throne of wind. I raise my arms above my head and feel the way the wind ruffles my shirt sleeves in imitation of raven wings. According to Norse mythology Odin, lord of the gods, had a raven perched on each shoulder. The ravens would awaken each day at sunrise, flying far and wide and across the world. The ravens would return each sunset, perch atop Odin's shoulders and whisper in his ears what they had seen. I stare at the raven hovering at edge of the Grand Canyon and wonder which of Odin's ravens I have met, Hugin (thought) or Munin (memory) when the wind shifts. The raven folds his wings into a different configuration, suddenly soaring across the vast expanse of the Grand Canyon in tens of seconds. I am left alone earthbound, standing on the edge of the Grand Canyon while the wind tosses my hair like flotsam and jetsam. I stand there and I dream of wings.

Gary Every

Raven Murder

Alone in the wilderness, far off any beaten path, I hear a raven calling "Caw Caw." A cry quickly answered by another black bird silhouetted against a pale blue sky. The ravens call back and forth as they soar above the long winding canyon. I amuse myself by thinking that the ravens are talking about me when the two crowing ravens are soon joined by a third, forming a triangle surrounding me.

"Caw Caw" cries echoing off the red rock when suddenly… there is a great cacophony of clatter up the canyon, a flurry of flapping feathers, as a cloud of big black birds, a coven of crows, a murder of ravens rise into the sky, wings wagging like the tails of hunting hellhounds, black beaks open wide as they fly and cry "Caw Caw Caw Caw Caw," rabid remarks barking up and down the canyon like a shrieking wind screaming about an approaching storm.

The unkindness of ravens do not rise in an orderly fashion ten… twenty… thirty… forty birds… swirl and soar, glide and dive, ride the winds like pirate surfers of the skies fifty… sixty… seventy… eighty black birds in the sky, tiny black thieves coveting bright and shiny things. There must ninety ravens flying high, circling and screaming, weaving in and out of each other in a loosely held cloud of black feathered fury and moving rapidly across the mountains, heading straight towards me. When the black cloud is directly above me all ninety birds scream at once an incredible chaos of chatter and then they climb over the canyon. The ravens have stolen the illusion of my silent forest and perhaps a piece of my soul because after all if those ravens have pick pocketed my immortal soul - wouldn't I be the last to know.

Vulture Mountains

"Where are we headed?" I ask, interrupting my toils as part of a claimstaking and surveying crew, bent over from my bundle of sticks like a medieval peasant retrieving firewood.

"Over there, towards Black Butte." Brian answers.

The air around the volcanic mesa shimmers with reflected heat, looking as if the temperature rose any more that butte would return to molten lava. It is the southernmost peak of the Vulture Mountains. Vultures are the only birds ingenious enough to figure out how to stay perched atop the black volcanic crags. They piss on their own feet.

It is hot. I am always thirsty. My shadow is etched concisely, burnt on to the sand like the chalk outlines police draw around fatalities. My responsibilities mean trudging across the desert floor laden with poles, shovels, axes, saws, hammers, maps, and little boxes filled with papers which claim stake the land in the name of whatever geological entity we are hired hands for; similar to wandering Spanish conquistadors planting flags and crosses in these same deserts many centuries ago. In the middle of the Mohave, Chihuahua, and Sonoran deserts, in corners so distant that even the wind gets lost; we triangulate and calculate. It is my personal epiphany of existential futility; using a geometric language whose abstract icons of angle and distance have little do with a terrain we are measuring into precise rectangles. It is the kind of existence which makes a man contemplate buzzard urine.

Gary Every

Some of the two dimensional Euclidean shapes we are surveying make no sense at all for the terrain. This day, one of our points is about thirty feet up a cliff and needs a tagged post hammered into it. We flip a coin and Lady Luck chooses me to scale the cliff. By the time I have returned Brian has discovered an eagle eye. An eagle eye is a small cave in a cliff where one can attain an outstanding view. We put down our bundle of posts and take an exploration break only to discover that this is not a cave at all but rather a hole carved into a free standing wall, a narrow sandstone facade on the cliff with a narrow ledge just barely big to turn around. The eagle eye is carved into the center. As soon as we scramble up into the aperture two hawks screech, circling above and challenging us. It is a magical eagle eye, the kind a shaman might use to survey a landscape of dreams.

Brian and I enjoy the view from the eagle eye, way up high in the Vulture Mountains and as we shift around the ground crackles and crunches beneath our feet.

This ledge is directly beneath the nest of the circling hawks who have littered the earth with their dinner discards. The ground is covered with a thin layer of sun bleached bones, squirrel skeletons and fragile rabbit skulls. The hawks screech again.

From the eagle eye we can see where the canyon dead ends, where canyon and chasm come together, cliffs rising up sheer on all sides. The cliffs also hold a large cavern. Brian and I decide to explore the cavern. We scramble past the talus and cactus to enter the cavern overhang. There is a distinct line, marking the bright sunlight and the dark shadow. On this blistering hot summer day we stop to enjoy the sanctuary of the cool cool shadow.

We stand there, breathless in the Vulture Mountain cavern, precious dampness clinging to the walls. Our eyes gradually adjusting to the darkness. Brian spies something and bends over quickly, shouting out "Feathers!" His voice echoes loudly in the cavern and there is a sudden burst of white.

In the darkness that burst of white is brighter than anything you can possibly imagine. That blast of white hurls itself at me and I duck. I turn my head, just in time to see a snowy white barn owl fling itself across the line of shadow and fly from the cavern mouth directly into the sun. This nocturnal creature wobbles as if it is momentarily blinded by the light. One of the screaming hawks drops from above.

Snaps the owls neck in half.

Then Brian and I see the other owl. This owl has the same snowy white feathers with brown speckles and glares at us, defending a nest with three chicks. We have accidentally killed a partner and mate. I cannot help but wonder if one parent will be able to raise three chicks in this bleak landscape. Perhaps we have killed the chicks too, only more slowly. We don't talk about it, just silently return to our job of carefully measuring random rectangles which do not quite fit the land.

Gary Every

The Petrified Forest

I love the gently swelling hills of the painted desert. Stripes of soft sandstone colors adorn the landscape, layers of tan, yellow, pink and purple flowing gently across the craggy landscape for miles. The rocks and soil are a combination of volcanic ash and sandstones deposited by marshes and creeks. All of it is brightly colored and erodes easily, crumbling into the most fantastical shapes. There are sections of the Painted Desert that could easily pass for the landscape of another planet or an exotic moon of Neptune.

On September 28, 1851, Captain Lorenzo Sitgreaves discovers a vast "petrified forest", so called because of the large number of petrified logs and pieces of petrified wood scattered about the area. On December 8. 1906, president Theodore Roosevelt designated this area Petrified Forest National Monument, the second national monument in the

United States. In his book <u>Roadside Geology of Arizona</u> Halka Chronic wrote, "The Petrified Forest is not really a forest at all, but a region where in Triassic time tree trunks rafted by flooded streams were buried quickly with stream sediments and volcanic ash, and later impregnated with silica and preserved. The great logs are almost all lying horizontally. Most are battered, with roots and limbs broken off and bark stripped away." The vast petrified forest is not the remains of a forest but the ancient debris left behind by a natural disaster catastrophe. In a caption to a photo Chronic speculates that the "logs of the petrified forest may have been uprooted by catastrophic volcanic explosions and transported by mudflows similar to those that followed the Mt. St. Helen's explosion in 1980."

The logs were preserved by a process known as silicification when bits of silica present in the volcanic ash slowly replaces the organic wood of the tree until only the stone remains. In the case of the petrified forest much of this stone is crystallized and agatized. Not only is the Petrified Forest in Arizona one of the largest collections of petrified wood but it is also one of the most beautiful and colorful. There reds, yellows, blues, and purples embedded in the stone trees, glisten in the sun like arboreal jewels. According to Christa Sadler in her book <u>Life in Stone</u> "Trace fossils interpreted as bees nests have been found in petrified trees at Petrified Forest National Park. If these features were indeed formed by bees, it would be the earliest true evidence known of bees anywhere on the planet and the earliest evidence of social behavior in insects." What makes this especially interesting is that this would mean bees existed long before there were flowers.

Gary Every

Of course the Petrified Forest has flowers today, small scraggly bushes scattered across the brightly colored hills. Those few flowers bloom brilliantly, forced to produce brightly colored blossoms to compete with the crystallized trees. Beside the flowers there are a handful of knee high bushes which dot the landscape here and there. This parched dry desert is a far cry from the humid tropical jungles which stood here during the Triassic when the petrified forest being formed. Then atop a red, white, and yellow petrified log I saw a color just as brightly attired with green, yellow, red and a white belly with black spots. It is a collared lizard.

When I show Lehi Bennally, a Navajo friend, my photograph of the collared lizard atop the petrified wood, he shakes his head and says he does not like these lizards. "They are fast," he says. It is true, collared lizards are fast. They must be they are predators of other lizards. Lehi said, "When me and my brothers were still little boys our father used to tell us that we must always be good runners fast and long. Good Navajo boys were good runners. Fast enough to run away from collared lizards. Not all white boys were good runners and you could tell which ones. Collared lizards would catch those little boys who were not good runners and would pee on their heads. Later, when they grew up - those little boys would be bald.

    This is reptile country with a wide variety of lizards and snakes living here. It has been reptile country for a long time and has the fossils to prove it. The Petrified Forest has been a treasure trove of fossils. As one would expect from a landscape of marshes, rivers and creeks one of most abundant fossils found in the region were those of prehistoric crocodile called a phytosaur. One of the more interesting fossils found in the region are the plentiful specimens of coelphysis. These graceful predators stood six to eight feet high, walked on two legs and held long trails out behind for balance. Sadler says "This swift agile creature with lightly built hollow bones had a long head with large eyes and sharp serrated teeth." These carnivores tended to run in packs and sometimes their gathered numbers grew so large that it might better be described as a herd. Coelophysis ate lizards, insects, and it is suspected that one of the main foods of Coelophysis may have been Coelophysis. In 1947, pioneer paleontologist Edwin Colbert was on his way to dig at Petrified Forest he stopped to inspect Ghost Ranch New Mexico. What he discovered there was so amazing that he stopped there. Literally thousands of complete and nearly complete coelophysis skeletons were preserved in a streambed layer of silt, victims of a natural disaster, perhaps similar to the one which flooded the forest with battered logs.

Loving our Arizona petrified forest so much when I visited the wonders of Yellowstone I had to visit their petrified forest as well. I remember discovering three trees. The biggest one had a fence around it as it crumbled back into the earth. It wasn't a wasted trip, my journey in search of petrified wood took me to the Grand Canyon of the Yellowstone where Yellowstone Falls is as spectacular as any I have ever seen.

Mountain man John Colter, a member of the Lewis and Clark expedition, Yellowstone during later explorations was the first to see Yellowstone . As Colter stood before Congress and tried to explain the wonders of what he had seen, majestic mountains, mighty rivers, hot springs, and geysers which erupted into the air, members of Congress were loudly skeptical. Catcalls and boos were rained down by the audience upon the nearly illiterate mountain man whom nearly all the senators and representatives assumed was lying. At last a frustrated Colter is reported to have shouted out, "I saw a petrified forest filled with petrified trees, where a petrified bird hung on a petrified branch and sang out 'tweet, tweet, tweet.'" Then the frustrated mountain man stormed off the stage.

The Bee Tree

I was hiking the rugged ranch lands and arroyos around the corner of the Rincon Mountains as the vultures circled and ravens cackled, following the winding stream which disappeared and reappeared traveling above and below the sandy soil when I heard a buzzing sound. There was a hum so strong and loud that the sky vibrated as I wound my way along the shallow canyon walls expecting to see a generator or water pump but definitely some sort of machinery.

What I saw instead was a huge palo verde tree with a green trunk as big around as a cow and the green branches wore tiny yellow blossoms. The entire tree (a HUGE palo verde) wore a canopy of yellow flowers and from every flower hung a bouquet of bees. It was more bees than I had ever seen. It was more bees than I could possibly imagine. It was more bees than there are in the whole world. Even though you are not supposed to because all the bees around here are Africanized killer bees, I approached the tree and sat beneath its shade.

God, there were a lot of bees, one on every flower and more flowers than I could count. I sat there and listened to their insect talk all day long, the hum of their wings vibrating the trunk of the tree. A bee landed on me, alighting softly on my wrist, and then soon there were two, three, ten, fifteen, thirty bees covering my person; shoulder, legs, and face. They tried to communicate to me in their secret bee language which scientists say consists mostly of dancing to express concepts of topography and travel but still it occurred to me to listen and see if I could learn what it felt like to fly. The bees squiggled across my flesh dancing their songs of floral topography but I did not quite understand.

When the sun was setting and the dark was coming, I arose from my seat and began the long walk home. To say goodbye to the tree of bees I danced a little jig but I suppose no one understood except a couple of cows - who chuckled.

While dancing I stumbled clumsily, nearly stomping on an old compass half buried in the ground. The compass was made by an old time cowboy from a spent shotgun shell and I still wear that compass around my neck, looped through an old rawhide string.

Now whenever I feel lost, I hum and dance until I find my way.

The Cross Eyed Sheep of Montana

Once I went canoeing in Lake Louise. Lake Louise is in the Alberta province of Canada. These are the mountains where they held downhill skiing events when the Olympics were in Calgary. The mountains are razor sharp and filled with glaciers so they are snowcapped even in the summer. Lake Louise is stunningly beautiful. Jasper and Banff are tourist destinations for people from the eastern part of Canada so everywhere you go in these hip little tourist towns people are speaking French.

Coming back from canoeing Lake Louise I had a summer job lined up for a few weeks at a sheep ranch in Montana. It made me a little extra gas money and gave me the chance to explore Montana a little bit. One of the most beautiful things I have ever seen was the full moon rising over Logan Pass on the continental divide in Glacier National Park. Once you get to Montana you realize immediately why it has the nickname Big Sky State. The sky is huge and vast and towers above you, stretching almost forever. You can't help but wonder why your sky back home is so small.

My work at the ranch mostly consisted of riding around on this tiny little motorcycle, fixing fences and manually moving the long rows of giant sprinklers which water the grazing pastures for the sheep. I would unhook a section of sprinkler and roll it forward, then go back and get the next section and then go back get another section and hook the sections back up. The main sheep herds were out in other fields and I really didn't mess with them much.

Gary Every

There was however one herd of mutant sheep and I dealt with them a lot.

The mutant sheep all had genetic defects. Defects that are common with all the inbreeding we force our domestic animals to endure. The herd of mutants consisted of about eighty sheep who were kept separate from the main herd. The mutant herd was led by a large billy goat. The billy goat wore a bell around his neck and was about three and a half feet tall. Plus he smelled sort of bad and had a most disagreeable personality. When you work on a ranch or a farm you quickly realize why the traditional image of the devil depicts him with two little horns and cloven hooves. It is no coincidence. Goats will eat anything, urinate on everything and defecate everywhere. They also like to knock you down with head butts. As soon as I met him the goat began nudging me with his head, testing my limits. I was warned not to tolerate this sort of behavior and it was best to wrestle the goat to the ground quickly. If I did not the goat would consider me to be just another mutant sheep and expect me to follow his lead. That was the one good thing about the billy goat, if you could convince the goat he had to go someplace, the determined goat made certain every last one of his mutant sheep followed.

There were two main types of mutations among the sheep. There were a few other variations but most of the mutant sheep fit one of two kinds. The most common sort of mutation caused a fifth leg to grow out of the center of the sheep's chest. The other common type of mutation caused cross eyed sheep. These were the dumbest looking sheep I have ever seen, which is saying something because sheep as a species are not known for their intelligence. For instance, during winter storms sheep will graze with their big fat padded fluffy butts facing the wind to protect themselves from the cold. In a bad Montana winter storm, sometimes the wind does not change directions for days. The sheep refuse to change directions, butts pointing into the wind and heads pointed the other way. If they keep moving forward for long enough the sheep eventually come to the barbed wire fences which border their pastures. If the wind does not change the sheep will just stand there until the snow starts to accumulate bit by bit, hour by hour until the sheep are slowly covered with snow and freeze to death. Stating that cross eyed sheep look dumber than other sheep is quite the insult.

It became apparent that the cross eyed mutation did have one distinct evolutionary advantage - the cross eyed sheep were extremely fast. The cross eyed sheep were fast but they sure did run funny. While facing forward, the cross eyed sheep skipped sideways, scissoring their legs adroitly, front and back legs kicking in synchronicity. They were really fast, much faster than regular sheep but if you chased them for very long, say seventy or eighty yards they would grow tired and dizzy. Then they would fall right over, panting on the grass. It was one of the silliest things I had ever seen and I couldn't help but chase them over and over again. Once, as I was chortling and laughing, the billy goat let me know he did not like me messing with his herd. He charged me. The billy goat rammed me in the butt with his horns and I was sent sprawling across the pasture. I still couldn't stop laughing, just lying in the grass and laughing while that goat stood above chattering away and cursing at me in billy goat language.

Kool Aid Tortoises

I love the desert tortoises we see rumbling across our Sonoran countryside. I often see the tortoises in some of our most rugged canyons and it makes me wonder if the tortoises are not better at scrambling over rocks and climbing cliffs than any of us could ever imagine. My favorite time to see the tortoises is when the prickly pear fruit is ripe. The first time I ever saw a kool aid torotise was while hiking in Esperero canyon west of Sabino and I was sitting by a stream minding my own business when a tortoise slowly came rumbling by - his face stained purple from eating the prickly pear fruit as if he had been drinking kool aid day long.

It was not too long after that I began harvesting the prickly pear fruit. I would handle them with barbecue tongs and drop them into big plastic buckets. Toasting the prickly pear slowly and evenly over a camp stove, just like toasting a marshmallow, was enough to burn off all the thorns and spines. Throw all the purple fruit into a big old vat and cook them down slowly over a low flame, stirring frequently. The pot should be purchased from a secondhand thrift store. The reason will become obvious after the purple fruit has been cooking for awhile. The inside of the pot will be stained bright purple forevermore. Reduce to a syrup and then strain through cheesecloth to remove the last of the thorns, seeds and pulp. I love hiking through the desert and drinking cactus juice. Back when I was trail running frequently and competing in races occasionally, I always filled at least one water bottle with a fifty/fifty mix of prickly pear juice and 7-UP. I remember one particularly long

Gary Every

beautiful hike/run when I returned home and my girlfriend giggled. "Your lips are purple. You look like you have been drinking Kool-Aid"

I smiled like a tortoise.

Burnt Turtles

There was one time when Barry and I went hiking in Saguaro National Monument just after a forest fire had scorched the desert floor. It was during a period of my life when I was fascinated by forest fires. I would drive around the state and take photos. Looking back on it none of the photos were worth a damn but it sure was exciting. Forest fires in the desert are a strange thing, and afterwards the ground is bare. Burnt cacti leave the most bizarre charred skeletons, especially the cholla and agave. Everything is black or ash white. This fire was so recent that the ground was very hot to walk upon. We were both carrying our cameras and snapping photos of burnt barrel cactus glowing like orange pumpkins, white ash cholla skeletons traced and laid out on blackened scorched earth. The ground radiated heat.

Then suddenly we saw a turtle lumbering across this apocalyptic scene. Not a desert tortoise but a turtle. He

Gary Every

was moving quickly as if the hot earth burned his feet. He
was panting. That turtle was in a world of hurt. When we
picked the turtle up his shell was hot. Barry and I took turns
carrying the turtle and we carried him for miles until we got
to a small desert stream whose granite bedrock had formed
a natural firebreak which had stopped the wildfire. The
south side of the stream was charred for miles and the
north side was Sonoran beauty in late spring, hummingbirds
hovering and feeding from the red ocotillo flowers. We
could hear the trickling sound of a small waterfall and
deposited the box turtle at the edge of the pool, wishing
him well.

Barry and I returned to the area just about a year
later, near the end of a really good monsoon season. There
were few traces of the fire to be found, a charred agave
stalk here or a scarred saguaro there. Grass and wildflowers
were everywhere. The grass grew about knee high and
covered the hillsides. Barry and I were delighted to see how
swiftly the earth had healed. We ran across the desert, just
happy to be alive, grateful to be so healthy. When we
came to the bottom of the hill where the grass was at it
thickest there was a tremendous noise. Barry and I stopped
dead in our tracks as hundreds of doves lifted up in a storm
of feathered wings flying beyond the hill in a dark cloud of
birds. The doves just kept rising and rising from the grass,
more and more doves with the tremendous roar of their
wings filling the breeze. It was so many doves they couldn't
all take off at once and had to wait their turns. The silence
that followed was deafening until Barry and I interrupted it
with raucous laughter.

We had been here just a little more than a year
before, wandering an apocalyptic scene of ash and fire.

Battling the Hydra

There had been a winter and then a wet monsoon followed, washing the layer of black soot from the soil and nourishing the grass which sprouted from the earth in leaps and bounds. In autumn the grass went to seed and the seed brought the doves. So many doves that they would not all fit in the sky at once, the roar of their wings loud enough to echo off the Rincon Mountains, faint echoes coming back like muffled laughter. I thought to myself, wow that is one hard working turtle.

Coyotes

A coyote suddenly went racing across Thunder Mountain Road. I wondered why it was running when a rabbitt ran across the road. Why was the coyote first? Was the rabbitt chasing the coyote? Then a second coyote burst across the road right on the heels of the rabbitt. I was watching two coyotes working together to chase down that bunny. Pretty impressive. Just as I was congratulating myself on seeing a really special moment and started to roll forward, a third coyote suddenly stepped from the curb and frightened by my car, stepped back into the desert. There were three coyotes chasing that poor rabbitt.

Native Americans believed that Coyote represented the Trickster and there are thousands of coyote stories. Maybe because they are so good at adapting and surviving in any environment. In fact the greatest density of coyote populations exists on the edge of urban environments, because they are so good at making raids on poodles and trash cans. You hear so much about species in danger of going extinct and animals losing range but coyote numbers have swelled dramatically and their range is increasing greatly with coyote sightings becoming regular in places like Washington DC where there have never been coyotes before.

When I went to Alaska, I remember standing outside the Tok Junction on the edge of the gorgeous Richardson Mountains when I saw a coyote and it looked just like an Arizona coyote. You have to understand all the animals look different in Alaska. We have deer and antelope but Alaska has moose and caribou. Arizona has badgers, Alaska has wolverines. We have black bears and so does Alaska but they also have polar bears and grizzlies. But when I saw the coyote in Alaska he looked just like an Arizona coyote.

Gary Every

Coyote Moon

To escape the summer heat
I hike beneath the light of the moon
taking forced breaks
whenever the lunar orb
is obscured by the cloudy monsoons.
As the hike stretches further into the night
my skin is caressed by a gentle cool breeze
carrying the dreams of countless civilized sleepers.
Far from the city
in the hills where I wander
the bats flutter like butterflies
singing sonar echoes of nightmares
which ricochet without pity
inside unsuspecting slumbering skulls.
I hike far past midnight
before returning home to my own bed
where I sleep soundly
and then awaken to my alarm clock
wedded to my workday routine
I step from my front door
car keys in hand
only to discover a coyote sitting there
beside my automobile
just beyond the steering wheel
as if he is waiting patiently for a ride
so I offer to take him wherever he wants to go
but he trots away
with that ludicrous grin coyotes often wear
believing that somewhere in my subconscious
his message has already been delivered.

Coyote Sunrise

The coyote roared
just as the first rays of sunlight
bent over the mountaintops
to illuminate
the modern cosmopolitan cowtown.
Standing in the middle of the intersection
ignoring all the stop signs,
the wild dog roared, barked,
yipped, yowled, growled and howled
letting loose with all the ferocious canine vocabulary
he could muster.
Domestic dogs hid in closets,
cats cowered beneath covers
and suburbanites were rudely awakened
from their slumbers.
Then just for the hell of it
the coyote roared some more.
While I fumbled for my television remote control.
the coyote trotted off
to wherever it is the wild things go
while we busy ourselves
with the foolish illusions of civilization.

Gary Every

Coyote Birth Control

This is an old story I sold many times many years ago, including to the joke page of Arizona Highways but it is not my story, this is an old cowboy joke. Exactly how old no one is certain but when I sold it to one western magazine somebody sent in a letter to the editor saying that they had heard the story in Wyoming in 1929. I hope you like it.

Once upon a time there was a parcel out west filled with a bunch of sheepherders that was having a terrible coyote predation problem. As the numbers of their flock dwindled the sheepherders went to the government requesting a solution to their problem. The government responded by sending out a university intellectual egghead bureaucrat kind of guy. The egghead called a town meeting and invited all the sheepherders to attend. The problem, he said, is that coyotes are sensitive breeders. The number of pups in a coyote litter can vary anywhere from two to fourteen coyotes; depending on the circumstances. Therefore it is almost impossible to eradicate the coyote population by hunting them. They just make more coyotes in a hurry. We can try leaving poisoned meat out but either the coyotes figure it out real quick or the ones that survive breed like rabbits.

Therefore, the university intellectual egghead bureacrat kind of guy presented a new sort of plan. To control the coyote population they would still put out baited meat but instead of poison the meat would laced with birth control. This would not result in an immediate decline in the coyote population but in the long run it would put a stop to the sheepherders problems.

To drive home his point, the university intellectual egghead bureacrat lectured on and on with lots of research cleverly displayed with charts and graphs filled with circles and arrows and little paragraphs on the back describing each one. While the dumbfounded sheepherders looked on, the egghead bureaucrat began to talk about coyote fertility by age, coyote love urges by elevation, coyote sex drive according to season, coyote romantic interest conveyed by the phases of the moon, coyote horniness by time of day…

At last one of the frustrated sheepherders raised his hand and interrupted the longwinded lecture.

"Excuse me sir," the sheepherder said, "All this talk about coyote romance is fine but when those coyotes catch our sheep all they want to do is eat them."

Gary Every

Grasshopper Mice

While I type, my cat sits in the window and turns her head, letting me know she is listening carefully. I know what she is listening for. Normally my house is filled with the noises of modern civilization, the hum of air conditioners, the nonstop blare of television and radio, the rumble of suburban automobile traffic. Today my house is unusually quiet and my cat is sitting, listening carefully for the strains of barbarism just beyond our domesticated home.

My cat is quite the urban hunter and sometimes I am devastated by the prey she brings home; lizards, birds, mice, baby snakes, and about every other full moon I wake up in the morning with a dead headless rabbit on my chest. It is like some sort of sick feline mafia joke; except my cat is giving me these gifts out of love. Today, she is listening for a quarry worthy of her hunting talents. My cat is listening for the howl of the grasshopper mouse.

Grasshopper mice were only discovered about twenty years ago in the southeastern Arizona prairie. Many people would be surprised to discover that Arizona contains vast expanses of prairie, mile after mile of rolling hills and grasslands; wine country, a home where the antelope roam. In the 1980's, there was an entomologist in all that grassland studying what else... grasshoppers. Every morning, the entomologist would faithfully check his traps and sometimes they were filled with grasshoppers and other times not. Sometimes the traps were filled with tiny mice. Lots of times. Every morning many of the cages were filled with annoying little mice. He would dump the mice and faithfully count his grasshoppers.

Being stuck in the middle of nowhere; an endless prairie where even the closest tiny towns are a long drive away and being a naturally curious scientific minded fellow, he eventually decided to identify the species of annoying mice. Flipping through his field guides he gradually realized that he had stumbled upon the discovery of a new type of rodent. The entomologist kept this news a secret, at least until the grant money for studying grasshoppers ran out. Then he applied for a grant studying this new species of rodent. Which I suppose is how scientists stay employed.

He cashed the check for the new grant, named them Grasshopper Mice and began investigating. They are amazing little rodents. The mainstay of their diet is grasshoppers and that is why the scientist was discovering them inside his grasshopper traps. Grasshopper Mice do not burro, build nests, or sleep in dens. Grasshopper mice are nomads. They follow the herds of grasshoppers as they swim through the vast oceans of prairie grass and when the day ends, they sleep in the nearest bushes. It is exactly how archaeologists believe the Clovis Men followed the herds of mammoths. Bands of mammoth hunters used to follow the herds of mammoths, sleeping wherever the giant prehistoric elephants stopped. It is almost as if the grasshopper mice are the true descendants of the very first Native Americans, the Clovis Men, this continents first human citizens.

Here is the amazing thing, like lions or wolves, the grasshopper mice hunt in packs. The hunting packs communicate by pounding their hind feet on the ground, beating the earth like a war drum. Some mice charge, fierce rodent warriors, chasing the swarms of grasshoppers to where other mice wait in ambush. The mice leap capturing their prey in mid-flight, grasping grasshoppers with tiny sharp claws. The mice pounce and their weight forces the grasshoppers to the ground. The entomologist bought one heck of a camera and ended up with all these close up photos of the rat pack gathered around the kill, resembling a pride of lions, green grasshopper guts smeared across their rodent faces. Then he got the most amazing photographs, pictures of the tiny mice faces, all of them with their mouths pouting to form little Os. The grasshopper mice were howling, tiny little mice howling together and celebrating the successful hunt.

No human being has ever heard the howl of the grasshopper mouse, but we have photographic proof it is out there. Apparently it is much easier to acquire a camera with an amazing telephoto lens than it is to purchase a microphone powerful enough to record the howl of the grasshopper mouse. It is a song of the wilderness which has yet to reach our hearts. Human ears have not yet been able to hear the howl of the grasshopper mouse but we have begun to listen.

Cats, with their sensitive feline ears might be able to hear the yowling rodents. It is what I believe my cat is listening for. Princess sits on the edge of my computer desk, with her head cocked, ears listening closely for sounds just beyond the edge of our suburban domicile. My cat listens for the howl of the grasshopper mouse, perhaps genetically remembering and yearning for the days when all cats hunted free, the days before the Egyptians domesticated the first feline. My cat listens closely for the howl of the grasshopper mouse - a quarry worthy of her talents.

I try to warn her, things may not be as simple as they seem. What if there is one grasshopper mouse who is particularly clever; a genius rodent who invents spear hunting technology? Princess sits on the edge of my computer desk, her tail twitching in anticipation but perhaps the balance of power has already shifted. Perhaps somewhere a genius Clovis mouse king dreams of building empires, gathers his rodent army, looks at the food chain and schemes of climbing higher.

Gary Every

Tarantulas and Tarantula Hawk Wasps

I love tarantulas. You have to respect a spider that can stay alive for twenty five years. The large furry spiders wander across the desert during the summer monsoons. Normally tarantulas stay close to their holes, traveling only as far as they need to hunt crickets and the other creatures they dine upon. During the summer monsoons the tarantulas begin to migrate. Partially this is because hard rains will flood their homes. A closer look at the migrating spiders will reveal that most of them have pinched abdomens that identify them as males. These migrating tarantulas are looking for love.

It is one of the most romantic pilgrimages in the animal kingdom. These lovelorn spiders will sometimes traverse the terrain for miles searching for a female. When the bachelor spider comes courting he approaches the females den which has a small web spun across the door. The male tarantula uses his fangs to pluck a love song on the strands of her web as if he is plucking out the notes of melody on the strings of harp. As if that were not enough while he is playing this love song all eight of his legs dance feverishly, performing a courtship dance for his potential bride. What female could say no to his proposal in the face of such love and devotion? When the lovemaking is finished the female devours the male. A few bachelor spiders are fortunate enough to escape and love again, but very few.

There are worse potential fates which await tarantulas. Sometimes, one sees black wasps with orange wings flying the desert skies. They are relatively harmless to people but for the tarantulas it is another story. This is one of the more gruesome tales in all of the animal kingdom.

The tarantula hawk will sting the tarantula and paralyze it. The skinny wasp drags the giant spider to a burrow and stuffs it inside. Then the tarantula hawk lays an egg on the paralyzed tarantula. When the young wasp hatches it will devour the tarantula bit by bit as the spider lies there helpless.

One day I was hiking in Sedona, taking the Sugar Loaf Trail beneath the shadow of Coffee Pot Rock, I saw a black and orange wasp dragging a paralyzed tarantula. I started taking photographs of the gruesome event. Two little old lady tourists asked what I was doing. I told them in gory detail. The old ladies were probably trying to discover one of Sedona's metaphysical vortexes, seeking spiritual enlightenment and here I was giving them nature red in tooth and claw. They left me alone.

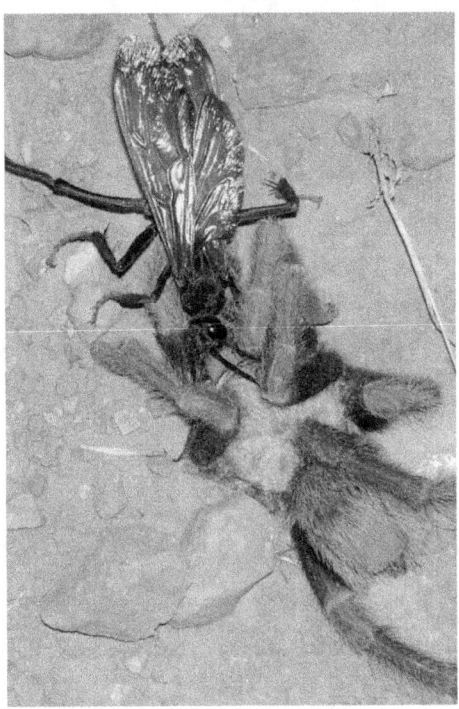

Giant Carnivorous Ostriches

Not a lot of animals hunt together, wolves, lions, grasshopper mice, and Harris hawks. One day I was driving away from Grandma's house and there were five Harris Hawks sitting in a mesquite tree. Harris Hawks are large black raptors with red marks on their shoulders. One or two of the birds will fly low through a thicket and scare up any quail, rabbit or other critters from the brush while the other hawks are circling above. The hawks in the sky have a birds eye view of the fleeing game and swiftly hunt it down. Later the birds share their meal while roosting together.

There was a prehistoric bird who used to live in the Americas called the Terror Bird. Terror Birds were huge twelve to fifteen feet tall, with tiny arms like tyrannosaurs and great big heads at the end of real long necks. The long necks held humongous skulls attached to giant beaks perfect for tearing flesh off the bone. These birds were believed to be very fast, perhaps running as swiftly as thirty five miles per hour, using the long necks and heavy heads both as ballast and as weapons. Here is the scary thing, terror birds used to hunt in packs.

Outside the little town of Picacho, Arizona is the Rooster Cogburn Ranch, home to the largest ostrich farm in the world. When Samantha was little and we had to drive to Phoenix for any reason we would always stop at the ostrich ranch. Sometimes Samantha's little cousin Sara would tag along and the girls knew that I would buy them as much bird food as they wanted as long as they ran. You see, the ostriches were used to getting fed and the giant gangly birds would approach the fence whenever anybody came close with a bag of ostrich grub. There would be these two little girls surrounded by hundreds of giant birds. Then I would shout "Go!" and the little girls would squeal and giggle as they ran back and forth along the fence, spilling bird food. On the other side of the fence hundreds of the giant birds would chase the little girls, tiny useless wings flapping madly and giant bird feet stomping on the earth like thunder as the ostriches stampeded. It looked for all the world like that herd of giant birds was going to hunt down those two shrieking little girls. I would laugh and laugh.

Gary Every

The Terror Bird Poem

Along the tip of South America
deep in the heart of the Patagonia Mountains
are countless fossil remains
including those of the terror bird.
Terror birds were giant carnivorous ostriches;
monstrous, flightless, birds of prey
who ran about at great speeds
on thick muscular kangaroo like legs.
Terror birds were nearly fifteen feet tall
with tiny tyrannosaur arms instead of wings
and here is the most amazing thing -
terror birds hunted in packs like lions and wolves
devouring all sorts of Pleistocene flesh on the hoof.
The Patagonia terror bird fossils
predate all known existence of man
and even the later digs in the land of Florida
are still older than the earliest human
but way down south in Texas,
in a silty stream bed layer
they discovered terror bird parts -
fang, claw, and beak,
which date back only 10,000 to 15,000 years ago
back to when fur clad, spear toting warriors
roamed the Texas prairie and plain
hunting the mammoth and mastodon.
So it is possible that terror bird and human
once met nose to beak
and you have to wonder who was the hunter
and who was the meat?

How different would our perspective swirl
how different would be our history of the world
if instead of butchering or hiding

Battling the Hydra

the Clovis men had domesticated the terror bird
and taken up riding.
What a surprise it would have been for Cortes
to have landed on Mexican shores
with his proud conquistador captains astride horses
armed with lances
only to face an Aztec cavalry armed with atlatls
and riding giant screeching, squawking, terror birds.
The Aztecs would have ripped
the conquistador cavalry to shreds,
left the Spanish soldiers for dead.

You have to wonder
what would have happened to terror birds
at the hands of the scientists of the Mexican highlands;
a people so adept at farming and genetic engineering
that over the centuries
with experiments in cross breeding
they turned a grassy weed like teosinte
into ears of corn;
the staple crop of entire empires.
After years and years and years
of domesticated breeding,
genetic manipulation and animal husbandry
they might have invented the flying terror bird.
Certainly Columbus Day would have a different meaning
if he had landed in America in 1492
and the fierce cannibal Carib
had used their terror bird army to hijack
the Nina, the Pinta, and the Santa Maria.
Imagine Spanish galleons sailing back to Europe
with crews of feathered Aztec warriors
riding flying terror birds
like planes taking off from aircraft carrier decks.
Imagine if the invasion and wars of colonization in 1492
had gone in the other direction.

Gary Every

The Summer of the Skunks

It was a dark and stormy night when I heard a rustling in the kitchen trash. Why was my cat digging through the garbage in the middle of the night? I shouted blasphemous insults, hoping to dissuade her mischievous efforts. The rustling continued until the entire garbage can toppled over. Reluctantly, I arose and flipped on the lights, strolling into the kitchen where I expected to give my cat a good scolding. Except it was not my cat rummaging through the kitchen trash - it was a skunk.

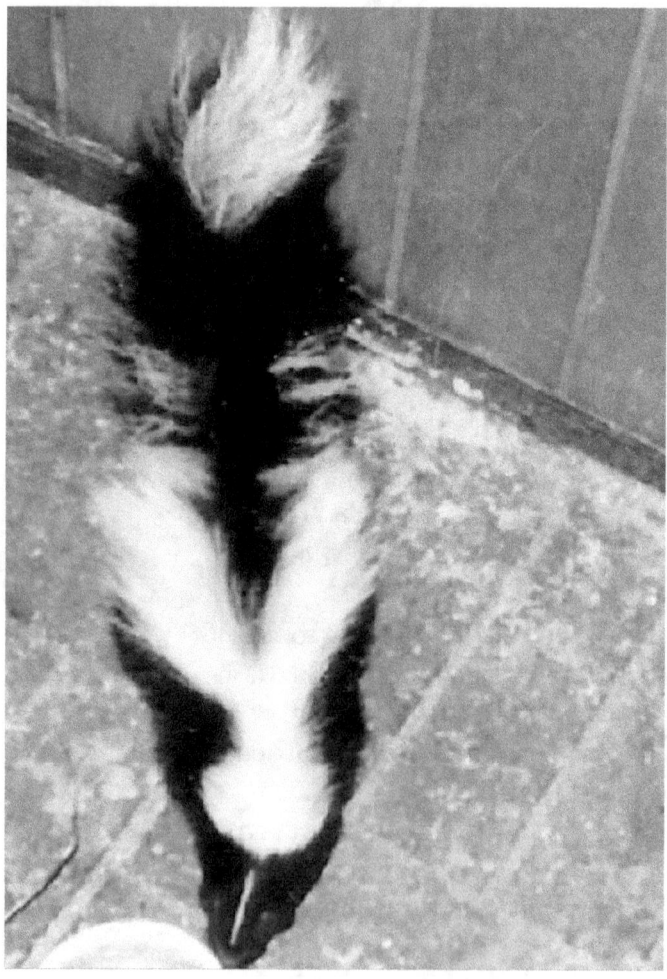

I was more startled than the skunk, who appeared calm, cool and collected. The skunk interrupted her dinner and slowly shuffled down the hall in that funny sort of waddle skunks have. The skunk seemed to be in no particular hurry. I followed the skunk, not real close, but I was curious where she was going. The skunk waddled down the hall and turned into the bathroom. One of the bathroom cabinets was open and the skunk slipped inside. I dared a peek just as the white plume of the tail disappeared down a hole in the floor. An opening had been cut to run pipes into the bathroom and the hole was just big enough to allow the skunk to sneak through. I was able to block off the hole with a small rock and thought that was the end of the skunk.

A few days later I began to hear soft mewing sounds underneath the trailer. I quickly realized that the skunk had denned up in the crawl space beneath my home and

given birth. I soon discovered that the stone blocking the hole was not big enough to keep out tiny little skunk kits. I woke up in the middle of the night and saw three baby skunks patrolling my bedroom. My cat was perched on the desk beside the computer and looked at me with an indignant scowl as if to say, "Dad, won't you do something about this."

Baby skunks are not born with the ability to spray their chemical weapons. They have to grow into it. I liked my trailer full of baby skunks, so I secured the kitchen trash and bought more cat food. Skunks are in the Mustelid family and their closest relatives are ferrets, otters, weasels and badgers. Both the badger and the skunk are plantigrades, which means they walk flat footed instead of on their toes. This is what gives both animals their distinctive waddling shuffling gait. Four legged plantigrades are very slow creatures but both badgers and skunks have effective weapons for defense. Badgers are just plain fierce. Built low and wide to the ground, badgers weigh in at twenty two pounds. Skunks have an even more impressive defensive arsenal. They are famous for their chemical weaponry. Skunks have the ability to spray their noxious odors about twelve feet and usually have enough fluid in their bodies for about five or six volleys. It is enough to dissuade almost any predator. The only wild animal to prey on skunks is the great horned owl; a creature with virtually no sense of smell.

The skunks appear to be aware of the potency of their weapon and are rarely frightened. They give several displays before they spray, including stomping their feet and raising their tail. The spotted skunk must do a front leg handstand before spraying. Even skunks do not like their own stench. Skunks rarely spray around their own dens.

Arizona is the only state in the Union where all four species of skunk native to North America can be found. On a long moonlit hike with Brian Corn, we stumbled across three of these species. The journey started in Sabino Canyon, followed the Phone Line Trail up into Sabino Basin and then dropped back down Seven Falls. The most common type of skunk is the striped skunk and that is the species which denned up beneath my Oracle trailer. It was also the first skunk to visit Brian and I on the moonlit hike. The striped skunk blocked the trail, with his back to us and his tail in the air. These obvious warning signs stopped us dead in our tracks. We waited patiently until the skunk waddled away.

Our next skunk was up a tree. The tiny spotted skunk, the smallest of the skunk species is the only species which climbs trees. We were fortunate to see a hog nosed skunk the rarest of the species. The skunk was not as fortunate that we had seen him. Near the end of the hike, where the trail crossed the road, the hog nosed skunk had been squished flat on the asphalt. The hog nosed skunks are named after their long bald noses. The noses are useful as the skunk forages through the leaf litter for worms, grubs, insects, and lizards. "All skunks are omnivores and opportunistic feeders" according to A Natural History of the Sonoran Desert "They eat anything from beetles, grubs, and grasshoppers to rodents, birds and carrion, seeds, and fruit."

The fourth type of skunk is also the easiest to identify - the hooded skunk. Not only does the hooded skunk wear a ruff of fur around his collar but the top of his back and his big fluffy tail are solid white. He was the only type of skunk we did not see on the moonlight hike.

There was this one night when I returned from a backpacking trip in Utah to my Oracle trailer. I was awakened in the middle of the night. I rolled over and saw one of the baby skunks standing up on his hind legs, with the front paws not quite reaching the top of the bed. The little skunk strained and stretched, reaching out to just barely touch me with the tip of his tiny nose, nuzzling my arm. I had forgotten all about the baby skunks living underneath my trailer until just that moment. Apparently the kits were impatient for fresh cat food.

As the baby skunks grew quickly, the amount of cat food they devoured grew exponentially. My cat continued to be greatly annoyed, perched atop the computer desk, taking turns glaring at the skunks and then glaring at me.

She is just lucky the kits were not spotted skunks because then they could have climbed that desk.

Although one of the skunks touched me, I never touched them, even though I am certain they would have let me. I was already afraid that growing up in my living room would make them too accustomed to human beings for their own safety. Several people advised me to capture one of the kits and keep it as a pet, even though it is illegal. Some people even gave me the phone numbers of veterinarians who would perform the surgery to remove the scent glands. By all accounts, skunks make wonderful affectionate pets but in the end I felt that the skunks had been born free and needed to live that way.

One night the trio of baby skunks decided they were finally big enough and tough enough to take on the kitchen trash. Working together they were able to topple the can, strewing garbage across my kitchen floor. I chased them a little more aggressively than usual and as the last of the baby skunks waited for his turn to head down the hole in the bathroom cabinet, he stopped and turned to face me. He stomped his little feet. He was warning that he was about to spray me. Of course I felt hurt and betrayed but none of that changed the fact that it was now necessary to block up the hole immediately. The baby skunks were all grown up and the den was soon abandoned. I noticed every dead skunk on the road and that time of year, as baby skunks leave the dens for the first time, there are a lot of dead skunks in the middle of the road. Automobiles are by far the leading cause of death among skunks. I hope my baby skunks are out there today, safe and okay. I have to

Gary Every

wonder since I no longer live in that trailer if the new
residents are ever greeted by any midnight kitchen
surprises.

Baby Snakes

We were so busy looking at the ground that it never occurred to us that the real danger would come from the sky. The dusty Death Valley soil was covered for hundreds of yards with baby rattlesnakes in every direction, squirming and writhing across the hill. It was like something out of a horror movie except all the baby rattlesnakes were only four or five inches long. Hundreds and hundreds of rattlesnakes writhing across that Death Valley earth, it was so incredibly awesome and so incredibly creepy all at the same time.

Rattlesnakes will often den together, dozens and dozens of rattlesnakes combining into a writhing ball of scales, fang, and forked tongue, twining and intertwining. Rattlesnakes will den for warmth, breeding and maybe even for companionship. Once while hiking the Tortilla Mountains outside Florence, Arizona I came across a den, maybe forty, fifty, seventy snakes swirling, sliding, bending themselves like an infinite number of caduceus strung together in constant motion. I honestly have no idea how many rattlesnakes were writhing in that giant pile and was not in the mood to patiently count them. Apparently, on that Death Valley steep slope we had stumbled upon a nearby den where several clutches of eggs hatched all at once.

The hundreds of baby rattlesnakes were exactly identical and they all moved in that peculiar twisting motion associated with sidewinders. They looked like diamondbacks but moved like sidewinders. I was to find out that all newly hatched baby rattlesnakes move as sidewinders for the first few days. The baby rattlesnakes were already armed with venom but there was no way they could bite through a hiking boot. There was no way the tiny little snakes could strike above the boot, they were just too small.

So we went about our business. We were working geology in Nevada, looking for gold. We were walking up and down the steep slippery slope at carefully measured intervals and stopping to take plant and soil samples. There was a pretty good chance we would find gold too, the other side of the steep ridge was The Old Bullfrog Mine. The Old Bullfrog had been a lucrative bonanza in the early years of the 20th century. The mine had closed for many years until they reopened it in the 1980s as an open pit operation.

We were walking up and down the slope, carefully measuring, labeling our plant and soil samples and most importantly trying to avoid the hundreds of baby snakes who writhed across the ground like sidewinders. They couldn't bite through our boots but reaching down to scoop up soil would be a stupid time to get bit. So like I said we were so busy doing our jobs and looking out for the baby rattlesnakes that we were focused on the ground. It never occurred to us that the danger would come from above.

BOOM!

Dynamite exploded in the open pit mine on the other side of that ridge. We looked up and saw rocks and boulders being flung high, high into the sky. What comes up must soon go down and the rocks fell back to earth. Some of the rocks fell back in the mine, but some crested the ridge and fell on the other side, falling on the slope like a home run hit over the park. Large boulders, bigger than coffee tables fell from the sky and landed on the slope, much further downhill than us, crashing back to earth with a thud and making the slope shudder. If it hit you in the head it would probably only take a baseball sized rock to kill you. There were hundreds of those and a dozen or two bigger than coffee tables. We put our hands over our heads and ran down the slope, screaming and squealing the whole way. Baby snakes had to fend for themselves.

Gary Every

Mendenhall Goats

Before I went to Alaska I never would have dreamed that a glacier could be so beautiful. The ice spirals and writhes, there are crevasses and spiked peaks. There are so many colors, blinding white, deep sea blue, turquoise blue, turquoise green and rainbow prisms. Every time the sun goes in and out of the clouds the entire field of ice changes hue. Different glaciers have different colors depending on what type of rocks they have been grinding up.

Mendenhall Glacier is outside Juneau and I remember standing on the cliffs above and looking down on this raging river which flowed across the top of the glacier. The river was maybe a quarter mile wide, filled wall to wall with foaming whitewater. The river just leapt out of an ice wall, the force of the water bursting through the glacier and racing across the top of the massive field of ice until it fell into a giant hole and disappeared forever. The temporary river was loud, so loud. The whole time we stood before Mendenhall, in the middle of the summer it was melting and you could hear giant chunks of ice the size of cars, houses, and tall buildings crumble and crash. It is incredibly stupid and dangerous to hike across such a glacier.

So there were Ranger Roy and I hiking across the top of the glacier, debating what a stupid foolish dangerous and reckless thing we were doing when we saw mountain goat hoof prints. Mountain goats are among the most sure footed creatures in the world. Surely they know what they are doing and certainly we would be safe following in their footsteps. We decided we could dare to hike a little further. It was incredible stomping across that ice, water which had been frozen ten thousand years ago and perhaps hundreds of miles away. The ice architecture twisted and writhed, impossible shapes rising up and away as they melted and sculpted and the colors! The entire glacier sparkled, wet with rivulets as the sun shone down. In places the ice was this impossibly deep blue. Sometimes the sun reflected off the ice so brightly that it hurt my eyes. There was one spot where I was surrounded by four walls of ice and the sun shone down, reflecting off the glistening white surfaces and I saw rainbows. I realized that if I spun around real fast that the rainbows would spin with me blurring in a circle.

We followed those mountain goat tracks for a long time, going slowly and cautiously until suddenly the earth before us yawned open into a great crevasse. The mountain goat tracks disappeared down the steep icy slope into a gaping chasm, just disappeared as if the snow had avalanched away beneath their feet. I tried a step, then two forward, hoping to get a glimpse down to the bottom. Instead my feet slipped. I scrambled back beyond the edge. We tried tossing stones down the crevasse but never heard them reach the bottom, just heard them ricochet from side to side. To this day I do not know if the mountain goats had an impossible path down somewhere deep inside the ice or if they fell to their death. All I know is that we carefully followed our tracks back to the car in nervous silence.

Gary Every

1 sheep 2 sheep 3 sheep 4

I used to take part in the Cabeza Prieta bighorn sheep counts. The Cabeza Prieta Wilderness and Bombing Range is along the Arizona/Mexico border between Nogales and Yuma. It is one of the driest deserts in the world. This region averages two to four inches of rainfall a year. In an area roughly the size of Connecticut there are no rivers, creeks or lakes anywhere. There are a handful of tinajas, rock depressions which will hold water year round. In this dry and arid landscape, volunteers such as myself are crazy enough to sit out here in the hottest weeks of the summer in the hopes of counting bighorn sheep.

I awaken just before sunrise and hike towards the wildlife blind. The trail wanders along the top of the narrow winding volcanic ridges, putting me at eye level with the ripe, red, organ pipe fruit. Organ Pipe fruit is my absolute favorite cactus fruit, juicy like a cross between a pear and a watermelon. The trail itself is littered with teddy bear cholla thorns and in the pre-sunrise darkness cactus spines stab me often. After losing the trail more than once I stumble into the blind. The tiny shelter is made of baling wire and saguaro ribs. The wildlife blind is perched way up on the precipice of the ridge where the soft breezes can keep it remarkably cool even in the summer heat. The summer heat comes and comes. I am supposed to dutifully report the temperature every hour but the thermometer is broken. All that is left is to wait for the bighorn sheep.

As soon as I crawl into the blind, readying my binoculars from inside my secret hiding place a hummingbird hovers outside my saguaro rib house, staring at me. The hummingbird mocks my hiding place and then flies away. So much for the secret presence of the undetected observer. You learn immediately that the animals know you are there. I sit and wait for the bighorn sheep. The sheep never come. All week the bighorn sheep fail to come. I go home disappointed, dehydrated, and sunburned but marveling at the unusual sparse beauty of the Cabeza Prieta landscape.

If I was a fool to volunteer to spend nearly a week sitting in the desert sun during the hottest week of the summer the first year; I must have been twice the fool to do it the second year. This time I surveyed the opposite end of the wilderness refuge - stuck way in the western corner. The western end of the Cabeza Prieta Wilderness Refuge is much drier and more desolate. The narrow dragon backed volcanic ridges are very sparsely vegetated, even the cactus are few and far between. The organ pipe cactus are nowhere to be seen. The name of the water tank where the wildlife blind was located is a good omen, Buck Tank directly beneath the rocky, craggy spire of Buck Peak. It is a barren landscape - so desolate it could pass for another world in a distant galaxy.

I awaken before sunrise and stumble to the blind. I know that my only chance of seeing wildlife is in the early hours of the day before the landscape has become boiling hot. The sun rises and I am visited by the usual suspects - doves, quail, oriole, vulture, and raven. For a short time an alligator lizard, a lizard who is a predator of other lizards enters the wildlife blind and observes me. The alligator lizard stares and stares at me as he scurries back and forth beneath the saguaro rib blind, probably debating whether or not I am too big for dinner. Light slowly creeps down the canyon walls until at last the whole ravine is engulfed in summer and I surrender any hope of anything else arriving.

Then I hear a clattering of rocks.

The rocks skitter and my heart starts pounding inside my chest. After two years, days and days of waiting, and hour after hour roasting in the desert sun, finally my patience is rewarded with the arrival of two bighorn sheep. A ewe and a ram approach. Using the techniques we have been taught for identification purposes I can guesstimate that the ram is about three or four years old, horns curling back just far enough to touch his ear. The ewe is a little older and the pair are probably mother and son. They cover the rocky terrain surprisingly quickly and then nervously approach the water hole; retreat, approach, retreat, approach. They sense my presence and stare at the blind - sniffing the air.

I stir in my chair and the ewe begins to flee, scampering up the talus laden slope. The ram stands still and watches. The ewe freezes part way up the slope and waits, watches, but nothing happens. She returns to the ram and leads the way back towards the water hole, slowly cautiously. This whole time I am supposed to be taking notes but my every movement seems to frighten the sheep who I suspect cannot see me enclosed in the shade of the blind but they seem to be able to hear and smell me. Retreat, approach, retreat, approach, the whole paranoid ballet takes nearly two hours as the sheep dance about effortlessly on the rocks.

For just a second, outside the rock overhang where the water hole hides, the shadow of the ram, curled horns, majestic head, is cast upon the rock in striking silhouette. It is a photographic moment which I did not capture on film, my camera sitting inside the case beside me. I did not need to take a photograph. The memory of the shadow of the ram, skull and horns silhouetted against the rock will be etched into my heart forever.

Gary Every

Big Sur Turkeys

I pull into the campground at Fernwood Campground in Big Sur. I love Big Sur, redwood trees and ocean. I was setting up my tent in a soft drizzling rain with a rare white albino redwood tree on one side and a small river on the other when fifteen wild turkeys flew over the river and landed on the shore about twenty feet from me. As soon as I got my camera out of the car the turkeys got real nervous and flew back over the river.

The next day was Thanksgiving and it was pouring rain but I went hiking anyways since I always go hiking on Thanksgiving. It was wonderful wandering through the forest of redwoods, giant trees climbing high into the sky, with their tops drifting in and out of the fog. Suddenly I heard gobbling sounds and began searching for the wild turkeys. They gobbled some more and I searched some more but the turkeys were nowhere to be found. Then it started to rain harder and I moved close against the bark of a giant redwood tree seeking shelter from the storm.

Splat!

The biggest bird turd you have ever seen landed right next to my shoes. I looked straight up above me and found myself staring at an enormous turkey butt. The turkeys were perched way up high in the redwood trees. It never would have occurred to me to look up forty or sixty feet into the air to search for the gobblers. Apparently turkeys fly a lot better than I thought.

I kept hiking, following the river towards the ocean when I stumbled upon an old resort long since abandoned with a dozen or so little cabins hidden in the woods. There was a storytelling stage at the ghost resort, slowly sinking back into the forest, stones covered with moss and it reminded me of when I was a bonfire storyteller at Miraval, two shows a week for four years. It inspired this poem which appeared in a magazine out of San Francisco called Poesis and was nominated for a Pushcart Prize.

Gary Every

Amphitheater

I am stalking wild turkeys
trying to capture the perfect photograph,
a big tom
with bronze feathers and bright red comb
but the silly pudgy bird proves elusive.
I turn deeper into the forest
traveling further and further
between the trees,
giant trees towering high above my head.
Gobbling calls haunt me as I walk,
turkeys roosting in the treetops.
hidden in the shadows,
until I stumble upon an old abandoned cabin
and just beyond that

a long forgotten amphitheater.
Here, the trees have been sacrificed,
sawed and planed to make boards
then nailed into benches
arranged in rows like church pews.
The little stage is made of stone
old geological bones
covered with moss and lichen,
a few rocks tumbled out of place.
How strange to stumble upon this location
while I am lost in the woods.
I consider myself a storyteller.
and stand on the stage,
words falling from my tongue
like newborn rain.
Gradually ghosts fill the pews,
a thousand faceless warriors
whispering dialogue of yesteryore
echoes of my hero's tale,
while ahead and behind me the river
continuously flows.

Soccer Circus

Lions roared, monkeys howled, and my left wing called for the ball.

"Pass it through!" He exclaimed.

An elephant trumpeted as a defender lunged and tipped my pass away. I chased the loose ball and collided with Bidjou, a large bear of a man from Cameroon. Bidjou grunted, swatting me away with a swipe of his big paw and sent the ball towards his fellow Cameroonian. May was built completely different from big, surly, Bidjou. May was barely five feet tall and maybe ninety pounds, seventy of which were smile. May was tiny and swift. It was easy to imagine his ancestors chasing gazelles across the plains of Africa. I sucked up my breath and ran back on defense. I hated chasing May.

Even as I ran, caught up in the adrenaline of the game, I wondered what the gazelles were doing at that moment. Next to the soccer field was the zoo and back in those days I was fast and couldn't look at the gazelles without wanting to leap into the enclosure and chase the swift creatures about. On summer afternoons we would play ball until the sun set, glorious colors filling the heavens. After closing time the zoo animals waited impatiently to be fed, tigers roared, bears bellowed, and the elephants trumpeted.

May passed to Hugh, a large Brit who dribbled till he shot wide, way wide, barely hitting the end line let alone the goal. A peacock screamed, shrieking in disapproval at

the ballhog. The peacocks were the only animals free to roam the zoo, everyone else was caged. I felt bad for the fast animals like zebras and giraffes, penned inside tiny enclosures. Once we played a soccer game at a local prison. It was fun, the inmates thanked us and thanked us but when a ball hit the razor wire it deflated before it hit the ground, and there was no mistaking where we were - inside a cage.

The checkered ball sails over my head, from a Laotian to a Brazilian, then stolen by a Canadian who passes it to a Dane. Back then, playing soccer in the states was an international experience and sometimes I feel sorry for today's generation of American athletes who experience nothing but suburbia.

I remember the time we played the circus team. Ringling Brothers phoned before the circus came to town and asked if we could get an all star team together. Before they played us, the circus team had tied the mighty New York Cosmos with Giorgio Chinaglia and the legendary Pele. Like the prison inmates, the circus performers were grateful for the game. I remember playing defense, marking my man while the ball rolled down the sidelines when suddenly my opponent performed a flying somersault, landing on his feet right next to me without breaking stride. This guy probably made his living on the trapeze and I was supposed to stop him if the ball came in the air. He smiled. Even the gazelles were jealous.

Gary Every

I Was Once a Turkey Jockey

My favorite race that I ever competed in was the Thanksgiving turkey races in California. I played soccer at Cal State Stanislaus and the schools unofficial nickname was Turkey Tech. This was because the original construction of the school was behind schedule and as the first day of classes on the opening semester approached and the tuition money had not only been collected but long since spent, the first semester of classes were held at the county fairgrounds. The science labs shared space with the turkey pens.

The Thanksgiving turkey races were a big event on the tiny college campus. There are so many contestants that several races must be run, each heat winnowing the number of racers until there a quarterfinals, semifinals, and the final race to determine who is the biggest turkey of them all.

One could win a trophy (shaped like a drumstick) by winning the championship turkey race or one could win prizes for the best costume. Many of the turkey jockeys wore costumes like the turkey races were the second coming of Halloween. The list of turkey jockeys included gypsy girls, pirates, robots, spacemen, harlots, and wizards. As a member of the college soccer team I qualified as a minor celebrity and when I was asked if I would like to participate of course I said yes. How many chances do you get to add an esteemed title like turkey jockey to your resume. I lined up for my heat, for my costume I wore my soccer uniform, including my soccer cleats. Each jockey was given a turkey on a leash. They were all white turkeys. Despite the leash, it was illegal to run like hell and drag your turkey across the finish line. It was important that the jockey be behind the turkey at all times or he was disqualified. The jockey must persuade the turkey be first across the finish line. To accomplish this act of persuasion the jockey is given a small whisk broom. A turkey jockey can either use gentle words of encouragement or enough curse words to make demons blush in his attempts to convince the turkey to run faster but the only way he is allowed to touch the turkey is using the small whisk broom to spank his turkey softly.

The starter's gun went bang. Someone screamed and fell over, pretending to be shot - a Turkey Tech tradition. Then the turkeys and their jockeys were off. My turkey was swift but not the fastest bird. We were trotting along in fourth place when we came to the first obstacle. With a gentle flick of wrist, my whisk broom tickled the turkey's butt and the turkey leapt in the air, easily clearing the hay bale. The formerly third place turkey balked at the hay bale and decided to stop and graze rather than run anymore, no matter how much his jockey pleaded. Me and my faithful steed - we were now the third place turkey!

The next obstacle was a bale of hay with a small puddle of water on the other side. The first place turkey leapt atop the bale of hay and stayed there, not liking the water. The second place turkey leapt atop the hay bale and the first turkey nipped at it. The second place turkey jumped backwards off the hay bale, his jockey practically beating it on the butt with his whisk broom to no avail. As my turkey approached the hay bale I flicked my wrist and gently tapped the turkey on the butt with my whisk broom.

Suddenly I realized that I had some sort of avian superhero as my turkey let loose with a mighty gobble, spread his stubby little wings and launched up and over the hay bale without ever touching straw. The turkey flew completely over the water puddle without ever getting wet. I, on the other hand was not so graceful. My back foot crashed into the puddle with a splash. This splash frightened all the turkeys behind us. My and my superhero companion easily won our first heat.

I had some time to kill before my second heat and when I replied I wanted the same bird, race officials laughed and released me into the turkey pen to select my steed. There in the middle of a couple hundred all white turkeys I could not tell the birds apart. Instead I went for the biggest bird I could find, hoping he would lead me to victory. The race started well. My large stallion fowl rushed into the lead and when we came to the first obstacle I gave him a gentle encouraging pat on the butt with the whisk broom. The turkey turned around, puffed out its chest, fluffed up its tail and pecked at my leg, biting my flesh hard enough to draw blood. It was not a lot of blood but it was blood all the same. I was taken aback for just a moment and while I was taken aback my turkey strutted back and forth atop the hay bale victorious in his own mind while the other turkeys raced past. I tried to coax my turkey forward but it was not how he saw the world. The other turkeys continued trotting. Dejected I sat down atop the hay bale, my head in my hands and dreams of someday winning the Kentucky Turkey Derby shattered forever.

Badger

When I was working geology I was often sent to Nevada. Nevada is classic basin and range. There are mountains on the horizon, (the range) and deep flat valleys in between (the basin). In Nevada the valleys between the mountains are so vast and flat that they look like the ancient prehistoric oceans they used to be. There is plenty of sandy beach, just no water.

One time Brian Corn and I were working in the middle of Nevada near a place called the Pectolas Hills. There was a hill out there, a little pile of nothing about ¾ the length of a football field and about thirty feet high. Turned out the little bit of soil covering the hill was sitting atop a lump of almost solid platinum. That is why the hill didn't wash away, it was all the platinum underneath. That hill was worth billions of dollars. I didn't get to make a billion dollars on that job but at least I got to see wild mustangs every day.

One evening, nearing twilight, Brian and I were driving to the hotel after work. It was a typical Nevada two lane highway, one lane going each way into both horizons, with nothing but sagebrush and small sand dunes on either side. Sometimes when we were driving along the long flat stretches of Nevada highway, Air Force jets would come screaming over the mountains would drive above us on the highway, practice strafe us, and then barrel roll back out of the horizon. If they had been serious we would have been a dead burning pile of wreckage. I had taken off my hiking boots and was massaging my aching feet when a badger suddenly ran across the road. Back in those days Brian and I had a deal whenever we saw animals I would hand Brian my camera and I would chase them back towards Brian so he could get a good picture. Brian stopped the car and I jumped out, running across the desert in my bare feet and began chasing the badger. It wasn't hard.

Badgers are not very fast. They have wide squat bodies sitting atop stubby little legs and all their feet point outwards in different directions. When badgers run the stripes in the middle of their back wiggles as if the front and back end are not completely connected. I was able to catch the badger pretty quickly even in my bare feet and as I started to circle wide to turn it around the badger suddenly stood up and roared.

I did not even know that badgers could stand on their hind legs but it turns out they can and it makes them appear much larger, especially with their arms upraised and claws extended. Of course badgers can roar but until a badger is roaring at you, with its red fleshy tongue wiggling inside a mouth filled with rows of sharp teeth you have no idea how loud they can roar. It was quite impressive. All I could remember seeing was muscle, fang and claw. That was one pissed off badger.

I pointed and shouted at Brian, "I hope you got that picture."

Cuz I was done chasing that badger.

Gary Every

Fishing at Page Springs

Page Springs is about twenty minutes from my house in Sedona, at a spot where Oak Creek is beautiful, thirty feet wide and ten feet deep. The banks are lined with big fluffy trees and it is beautiful in the autumn when the leaves turn gold and red. There are a pair of kingfishers who live here and I have seen black hawks, ducks, raccoons and geese. Once while I was standing in a thicket of Himalayan berries a bald eagle flew about fifteen feet over my head.

One day as I strolled along the shore I passed by two fisherman. I offered a friendly hello which they returned. I came to a shallow waterfall where I spied a blue heron. The heron was wading between the rocks and while I watched the heron caught one, two, three trout. Each time the heron stood still, occasionally moving its neck at odd angles, and the head would dive forward and the long slender beak would stab into the water, returning with a trout writhing in its beak. It was amazing that bird stayed so skinny catching so many fish so fast.

As I returned to my car (after eating my fill of Himalayan berries) I passed by the two fisherman and asked how they were doing.

"Nothing all day." said one.

"There is no fish in this river." said the other.

The heron had a different opinion.

Fishing with Flowers
(For Russell Corn)

Copulating dragonflies hover,
eight sets of insect wings flying
like an aeronautical infinity sign.
Bluegills shimmer in the green water.
Walking by I frighten a white butterfly
atop a white buttercup flower.
A dear old man once taught me
to run a hook through the flower,
fly fishing with a flower instead of feathers.
All afternoon I bait and cast with flowers
strawberry four o'clock, morning glory and blue lupine
even parry's preposterously pink pestenmons
dangle from my line.
The murky mud is marked with river otter tracks
like the felonious footprints of floating fish stealing ferrets.
Then there is the bird, a big giant bird,
a humongous black and white bald eagle
who leaps from the cliff above us
and barrel rolls above the river
His broad shoulders flapping powerfully
as they carry him to a precarious stone perch
high above the water.
Our baldy buddy hangs out all day
and when I creep closer for a photograph
I discover a discarded feather,
a giant feather belonging to a giant bird of prey.
The Native Americans say an eagle feather
will carry a man's prayers directly into heaven.
I bend down to pick up my treasure
and save my wish for another day.
Today,
as I throw another flower into the wind,
I am feeling sort of fulfilled.

Herons Fill The Sky!

I have noticed lately that blue herons fill the skies,
sailing above desert, valley, and mountains.
The giant birds migrate, following riparian ribbons,
connecting lakes, rivers, and ponds
as they follow the changing seasons.
Long, slender, and angular;
the lengthy blue feathers stretch
as the wings unfold;
the shoulders powerfully beating the air
before the wings return to the flying beasts side
making the airborne avian resemble a streaking blue arrow.
I have never seen anything so graceful
as when herons fill the sky
and it occurs to me
that maybe they aren't flying at all
but merely hovering
as the earth spins beneath them
the seasons gradually changing.

Vashon Eagles

One of my favorite parts of visiting Seattle and my
friend the Wizard Crystal Fart is riding the ferry boats out to
his home at Vashon Island. The ferry boat ride takes twenty
or thirty minutes and I love to watch the luminescent
jellyfish float in the cold dark deep water. The wet forests
are filled with bright yellow banana slugs. Wherever you go
in Seattle, Mt Ranier hovers, glowing and white, and always
with clouds at the base so it seems to float above the
ground. Once I was hiking Mt. Ranier in July and hiked until
the snow got waist deep. I was forced to turn back because
of the waist deep snow. The next day I got off the airplane
in Tucson and it was 105 degrees.

Every time I visit the Wizard Crystal Fart I work on his
broken down bicycles, repairing them until they are road
ready. I spend much of my vacation bicycling around the
island and hanging out on the many beaches. The wizard

jokes that the nice thing about living on a small island is that
you can't lose pets. Where are they gonna go? They all find
their way home eventually. The island is steep and hilly so I
get in pretty good shape as I huff and puff the uphills and
relish every rapidly descending downhill. The island is
covered with large estates, horses, sheep, and beautiful
gardens with sunflowers and artichokes towering above
your head. The bicycle winds along twisting roads of forest
and seashore; rolling past flower gardens, horses, cows,

chickens, goats and even the occasional llama. There are pastures, meadows, wooden covered bridges and red barns.

The first wagon train pioneers to reach the Pacific coast were not trying to expand the reaches of Manifest Destiny but arrived because they were seeking a fresh start. The newspapers of the day were filled with stories of swindling land speculators, fraudulent bankers, and corrupt government officials. These early homesteaders felt that the ideals of the founding fathers had been betrayed. These Oregon Trail pioneers loaded all their worldly possessions into rickety wagons, heading for the Pacific shore where Thomas Jefferson's dream of a nation composed of gentleman farmers could be realized. They called their new country Jefferson.

It was quickly squashed with military force.

The highlight of the summer, every summer I have ever visited Vashon Island is the Strawberry Festival with a parade led by tots on trikes. There are old cars and horse drawn floats, beautiful hippy girls with painted faces. Once I paid five dollars to have my picture taken with a young woman dressed up as a Klingon. It was a fundraiser for the local humane society but that wasn't why I did it. I paid five dollars to have my picture taken with a girl dressed up as a Klingon because Klingon women are hot! The star of the parade was the island grocery store shopping cart drill team whose goofy enthusiastic intensity as they moved, weaving in and out of geometric patterns reminded me of intricate marching band maneuvers and suddenly I felt right at home. Vashon is the realization of Jeffersonian democracy, everyone a gentleman farmer, philosopher, and artist.

Gary Every

Culitivated parcels of land bulge with crops, lettuce, kale, carrots, turnips, tomatoes and blueberries. Many of these gentleman farmers make a little bit of money by participating in the underground economy. These tye dye rebels grow budding green crops with names like booberry, chronic cake brain, and frankenstone. The residents of this little island believe "We hold these truths to be self evident; that all men are created equal and endowed by their creator with these rights, life, liberty, and pursuit of happiness", that these words are more than just a pipe dream

There was one time I was standing on Sunset Beach, facing west , and watching a kingfisher fish the surf, hovering above the rolling waves. I looked up and saw a bald eagle flying directly towards me. The bald eagle was flying over the ocean but was coming at me at such an angle that it appeared he was flying directly out of the snowcapped Olympic Mountains on the horizon. Even at the rapid speed eagles fly, the eagle was far enough away that it took ten or twelve minutes to approach me, covering a vast stretch of open ocean and then just like that his white head and black body passed over me and he flew away, giant wings beating loudly, the echoes of revolution flapping on the wind.

The Multiverse

The Canadian geese awaken me at sunrise, flying low over the forest, following the bend in the river and honking to beat the band. I am cocooned in my sleeping bag, camped atop a picnic table in the Manitoba province of Canada, looking up at hundreds of goose bellies as they soar over head. The sunlight slices through the forest mist as the geese sing, greeting the day. It is the best alarm clock ever.

As a small child, about four years of age, I was once terrorized by two geese. Mom had dressed me in my Sunday best and I was walking along the edge of Randolph Park Lake, feeding the ducks popcorn. Suddenly, two large geese waddled swiftly towards me. The geese were much taller than I was at the time and they began to bully me, working as a team. One goose would bite me with it's hideous orange beak, chasing me around in screaming, frantic circles, while the other bird would gobble up all the spilt popcorn. My parents were laughing too hard to help me. It was horrible humiliating and terrifying besides.

The people of the Cheyenne, Arapaho, and Sioux, were continental citizens, making migrations that put them in the best parts of North America during the best parts of the year. Geese are also continental citizens, with no respect for international borders, continually chasing the tilt of the planet. The geese make an amazing journey, storing all the corn and sunshine that their feathered bodies can hold, and hauling it north to the arctic spring where they nest amidst crevices of ice and silence, manufacturing newborn goslings from all that stored solar energy

Gary Every

I remember one hot summer afternoon that I was fortunate enough to spend in Montana. I was walking along a marshy lake, spooking up waterfowl - duck, heron, crane, kingfisher, and loon - when suddenly I came upon an elderly gentleman fishing without a pole. He was a Native American, and I assume a Blackfoot because I was on the Blackfoot reservation but you never know and besides I did not ask.

He told me that the bird his people most revere is not the eagle, but that they consider the most sacred of birds to be our web footed friend - the duck. The Blackfoot admire ducks because of the long seasonal migrations which they undergo. Like geese, ducks are continental citizens, following the spring thaw and autumn harvest. The Blackfoot reason that seeing so much of the world must make the ducks wise.

"And another thing," he said to me as I was about to leave, "I do not live in a universe. I live in a multiverse."

That Manitoba morning when the low flying geese woke me up after the echoes of their song faded into the white water roar of the river, I sat up. Watching the geese fly into the heart of the sunrise; I was startled to discover a line of tiny muddy footprints, the trail of a small beast, a mammal, the size perhaps of a squirrel or weasel, leading from my toes to my head. While I had been sleeping some wild beast had crept across my body, stared into my eyes, tasted my breath, and maybe even read my dreams. For a brief moment I wondered if this wild beast found my dreams to be either inspiring or mundane, or if my civilized wishes were even understandable to this wild cousin.

Battling the Hydra

I am awakened by this flock of geese flying overhead our paths intersecting for a brief moment in the sunshine mist of a Manitoba morning. Sunlight paints the earth. I have no idea of where the geese have come from or where they are going, just enjoying my beautiful alarm clock. I too live in a multiverse.

Gary Every

Dead Man's Cave and Vampire Bats

Sonoita Arizona is a tiny town surrounded by grassy hills, cattle ranches, wineries, and antelopes galloping across the plains. Just south of town there is a small round hill that looks like any other hill except this one is hollow inside. This is Dead Man's Cave. As caves go it is not especially big or deep or beautiful but what makes Dead Man's Cave interesting is the paleontology. Dead Man's Cave is filled with fossils. While spelunking Dead Man's Cave as the flashlight shines across the mud walls the walls are filled with bone fragments. All the bones date from the Pleistocene which is the period of geology when the world was deep in the Ice Age. Fossil skeletons of saber toothed tigers and a rare prehistoric owl are only a few of the specimens that have been excavated from Dead Man's Cave.

If Steven Spielberg knew about all the cool animals that roamed North America when the continent was filled with mega fauna he might have never made dinosaur movies. There were mammoths and mastodons. A two hundred fifty pound tortoise roamed Arizona. There were several types of saber toothed cats including the scimitar cat which specialized in hunting mammoths. There was a North American lion who outweighed his present day African counterpart by hundreds of pounds. There were cheetahs here chasing the antelope and back in the Ice Age there were several types of antelopes including one that had four horns, one for each corner of its head, and a fifth horn that grow off its nose and forked. There were camels and horses, both animals migrating the opposite way across the Bering Strait to Siberia. There were packs of hunting terror birds. There was a short faced bear who was much taller than today's grizzly. There were long horned bison, tapirs, and shrub ox.

There was also a giant ground sloth that stood upright maybe twelve feet tall, weighed nearly a ton and had claws almost a foot long. The giant ground sloths were herbivores. They grew so tall in order to grab the trees way up high. They were strong so they could pull the tops of the trees down to their mouths and eat the tender shoots and leaves. It certainly did not hurt to be so big and strong in a land filled with lions, tigers, bears, cheetahs, jaguars, wolves, and terror birds. I read a paper by an archeologist who speculated that the giant ground sloths probably smelled bad. His reasoning was based on two premises. The much smaller slow moving sloths who still live in Central and South America are often covered with fungus and mold which gives them a rather unpleasant odor. Biologists believe this makes them distasteful to predators. The archeologists other premise was based on excavating the hearth and homes of the Clovis men, the spear toting hunters who spread across the Americas like wildfire. The Clovis men were very successful and apparently very hungry. The bones of just about every Ice Age animal are found in their fire pits except for giant ground sloths. The archeologist speculated that maybe the giant ground sloths smelled bad and this is why the Clovis men never ate them.

So nothing never ate the giant ground sloth? Nature doesn't work like that. In the Rincon Mountains east of Tucson there is Colossal Cave a tourist trap famous for its beautiful stalactites and stolen stagecoach gold buried somewhere inside. What many people do not realize is there is a second cave in the area Arkenstone Cave which is filled with fossils. Two spelunkers were crawling deep inside this largely unexplored cave when they came upon a room filled with bat bones. Upon closer inspection back at the lab, the scientists realized the prehistoric bat teeth had grooves. The grooves were for drinking blood. They had stumbled upon a room deep in this cave that had once been a home to prehistoric vampire bats! There were the bones

of other animals in this room as well - giant ground sloths. There is only one other place in Arizona where fossilized vampire bat bones have been found and that is the Grand

Canyon. Once again, the vampire bats were sharing the cave with giant ground sloths. Apparently there was indeed an Ice Age predator who fed from the giant ground sloths and it was the vampire bats.

There is an interesting lost treasure story associated with the vampire bats. There was a rumor circulating around that Father Kino paid for the building of the beautiful mission at San Xavier with a lucrative gold mine that was hidden nearby and since lost. The gold mine is supposed to be somewhere in the Baboquivari Mountains and those who wish to discover the hiding place need only prowl around the rugged slopes of this sacred mountain on a full moon night and wait for flocks of vampire bats to fly out of a remote cave. This is the cave where the gold is located. It is protected by vampire bats! At least that is the legend and by the way you might want to sleep with your windows closed tonight.

Gary Every

Ventana Dreams

Trumpeting trunks of wild wooly mammoths and the yodeling yowls of saber toothed cats still echo between these mountains even if the valley is now filled with nothing but cactus and creosote. There are no longer mammoths here but there are plenty of giant green saguaros. Many of the saguaros hold large bird nests to their bosom, bundles of sticks crammed between green arms and green trunk. These huge nests belong to giant birds of prey, hawks, owls, and falcons. The raptors feed on the tiny animals which scurry between the prickly pear and the scrub brush, jackrabbit, lizards, and snakes. There is not much big game in this harsh dry landscape anymore.

Such was not the case 10,000 years ago, when the Ice Age was receding. The glaciers never reached southern Arizona but the precious moisture did. This same valley composed of cactus and creosote was once filled with marshlands and lakes. The earth thundered beneath the hooves of the giant beasts who lived here then, mammoth, mastodon, camel, horse, and a giant bison with long curved horns like Texas cattle. The predators who hunted this giant game were huge, fierce, and fast, lions, tigers, and bears, oh my, jaguars and wolves.

Just like the dinosaurs, some scientists now believe that the mammoths demise was at the hands of extraterrestrial events. Paul Firestone of Berklee Labs has proposed a theory that a distant supernova 41,000 years ago began a series of cataclysmic events which changed the weather for the entire planet, causing the end of the Ice Age and the extinction of all the mega fauna in North America. The debris from this supernova didn't just hit our planet once but repeatedly in a series of shock waves 41,000, 38,000 and culminating 13,000 years ago when a nine mile wide comet landed in what would someday become Texas. The effect of this astronomical calamity was a period of global warming causing the Ice Age to end, glaciers retreating back to the polar ice caps.

Ventana Cave where the mammoth hunters once lived is on the O'odham reservation, where particularly brilliant meteor showers are recorded on O'odham prayer sticks going back centuries. The Apache have oral histories of spectacular shooting star seasons which date back hundreds of years. If Firestone is right, Arizona's Clovis men would have been present for this last shock wave of supernova debris. These big game hunters would have seen the streaking fireball as it burned through the atmosphere, maybe even seen it for days, screaming cataclysmically towards the planet. They must have felt the wind from the shock wave as the comet struck Texas, the force of the impact so incredible. Of course it would not have been just one comet hitting the earth but entire firestorms of meteors every single night. Sometimes there must have been several shooting stars at a time lighting up the nighttime sky. Shooting stars so bright they shone even during the daytime. The meteors crashing so close, one after another, that the booms were deafening, the earth shaking beneath their feet. I imagine the great number of shooting stars crashing into this lush landscape must have started many simultaneous wild fires, smoke billowing from several different forests at once. All the soot in the air would have made incredible sunsets, a panoramic anthem for the end of the world. Was there one mammoth who raised his head skyward, lifting his giant hairy elephant skull to look into a sky full of shooting stars, trumpeting a soulful wail on his trunk, a sad jazz song of extinction?

Reservation roads are never big on signs and the O'odham nation is no exception. I suppose it helps to keep the tourists away. I found Ventana Cave while I was busy looking for something else when on the edge of the Castle Mountains, I saw one of the largest rock windows that I have ever seen. This rock window is huge and suddenly I remembered that the Spanish word for window is ventana. I knew that Ventana Cave must be somewhere nearby.

I have only hiked out to the giant rock window once. It is miles and miles from the road, a long and arduous hike. I began at a roadside shrine, little brick altar and crosses erected in honor of a fatality. On the horizon the distant rock window is tiny. I traverse ridges, climb in and out of gullies, stumble on the talus and scree. The whole time the rock window grows steadily larger. The hike takes hours, my shoes fill with sand and my hands fill with cactus thorns. There are beautiful little crystal geodes littering the ground and soon I fill both my pockets.

The window grows continuously nearer while I walk and walk, slowly becoming larger and larger. The weight of the stones in my pockets causes my denim pants to sag beneath my waist and I am forced to hitch them up over and over again. I hike across this patch of ancient holy earth, stuffing my pockets full of worthless bright and shiny stones. The little stones grow so heavy that my pants sag and the top of my ass sunburns. The last slope to approach the giant rock window is steep, steep, steep, forcing me to pick a path between volcanic boulders and saguaro cactus.

Up close, the rock window is enormous, dominating the horizon, desert sunlight pouring through fiercely.

It is easy to stand atop the rugged ridge, staring through the rock window and pretend that geological aperture is a shaman's window. My eyes are dazzled by the stream of dreams riding sunbeams through the rock arch, like visions passing through the eye of a needle. I stare directly into the heart of the Castle Mountains, an ancient volcanic mound with a gash near the top, which was once a vent exploding with gases and magma and then became a cave, a very special cave, one of the first outposts of human civilization in Arizona over 10,000 years ago, home of the big game hunters.

It is so easy to stand on this ridge, panting and out of breath, and imagine the world as it might have been 10,000 years ago when the hunters awakened at sunrise and stood at the mouth of the cavern with weapons in hand, watching the herds of giant game thundering along lakeside shores. Fathers, husbands, sons, and brothers would plot and plan which hills to stampede the animals between, in which gullies the warriors would hide with savage cries, pointed blades, painted bodies, and wait for avalanches of flesh on the hoof - deer, antelope, camel and horse. Celebrating the meat of the feast with a roaring fire, beating drums, voices rising in howling song and the Ventanans scare the hell out of all the wild animals for miles around.

Of course it is just as easy to imagine this rock window 10,000 years ago with a shaman standing on the other side. He would have been a wild looking man with long black hair, dark brown skin, wearing a loincloth, bones and gemstones stuck through his nose, lip, and ears. Did he ever stand high on this mountain ridge and stare through this giant rock window, watching the glorious colors of the setting sun, the night sky gradually darkening, interrupted by shooting star after star, meteor after meteor. Did he ever stand in the middle of his Ice Age apocalypse and wonder what tomorrow might bring. As I stand there staring through this rock arch, trying to imagine 10,000 yesteryears, did this Clovis shaman, his body covered in tribal tattoos, once stare through the Ventana arch and try to imagine the future? Did he see me?

Look there goes a shooting star.

The wind howls through the stone ventana, whining like the wailing of a trumpet The light from the streaking meteor fades quickly, better make a wish fast before the darkness comes.

Gary Every

The Petroglyphs at Red Tank Draw

If you weren't expecting to see the petroglyphs it would be easy to hike right past them. To reach the petroglyphs you hike upstream, striding against the current of rolling boulders. The canyon meanders as it winds uphill, the canyon walls slowly close, red rock cliffs towering above. Water trickles atop the bedrock floor through a narrow passage known as Red Tank Draw. Then the canyon widens; splits, and the petroglyphs suddenly appear. These rock art pictures, only a short distance outside Sedona, Arizona, belong to the Sinagua culture; ancestors of the Hopi, Hualapai, and Yavapai peoples and date back to 1200 AD. There must be a reason why the petroglyphs appear in this specific spot and nowhere else up and down a canyon which stretches for miles and miles.

Three red rock boulders are adorned with Native American rock art. One picture panel in the center dominates the proceedings; filled with astronomical symbols, spirals, mystical beings, and a herd of magic deer. One of these deer, or perhaps it is an elk, is easily the largest figure depicted. The body of the giant elk is football shaped with four legs, a crooked tail, and a lower lip which juts out in a bovine way from the long snout.

It is the antlers of the giant elk which are the focus of attention. The antlers rise and branch; expanding, extending, and spreading outwards like dozens of fingers reaching across the landscape. The impression of the antlers is unmistakable to anybody who is familiar with maps. These antlers branch exactly like a river delta. This giant elk carved into stone is describing features of geology.

Other symbols are written into the rock; spirals which can denote direction or migrations. Spirals may also represent an inward spiritual journey on the metaphysical level. Round fat figures are pecked into the rock,

resembling horned toad men. These horned toad men have their arms bent upwards as if they are boasting, flexing their muscles and showing off their round full bellies. One stick figure man is wearing a headdress which makes him look alien and other worldly. His fingers and toes are drawn precisely but impossibly large, four fingers on each hand. One symbol can be identified from the Aztec codices, comprised of a cross surrounded by an outline; a symbol which stands for the planet Venus otherwise known as The Morning Star, one of the most important astronomical objects in Native American mythologies.

The most numerous symbols carved into the rock are the hoofed animals; deer, goats, and elk. The animals in this picture convey a sense of motion. The petroglyphs start with the elk in the lower left quadrant as the herd slowly rises across the panel in a clockwise direction. The rock art animals climb upwards, arcing across the top of the boulder, all the animals facing in the same direction, marching across the mythic landscape together. In the upper corner of the petroglyph panel there is a shaman in an antlered headdress copulating with a deer.

One has to wonder, why this is the only spot in the canyon where rock art appears. At first glance, there is nothing about this place which appears sacred. It is here that the canyon begins to widen, the rock walls lower, until gradually the sheer cliffs are replaced by small rounded hills. It is here that the canyons divide, redivide, and subdivide into dozens of little rivulets. The canyons, arroyos, and shallow gullies crisscross the desert hills. From the sky I would expect the branching of canyons to resemble a river delta drawn on a map or the antlers of an elk etched into a petroglyph panel.

Native American culture had a tradition of communal hunts. People would spread across the countryside in a giant circle. The circle would cover every direction for miles and miles. Men, women, children, and elders would take their places; beginning to bang sticks, pound drums, shriek, and whistle as they moved slowly forward. Gradually the circle closes, one step at a time, the people beginning a slow, loud migration towards the center.

Confused and frightened by the din, the animals flee as if escaping a flood of demons. First the small animals, jackrabbit and cottontail dart from the scrub brush. Larger game animals like deer, antelope, and javelina startle from their beds and burst forward. People shake rattles, bang drums, and shout, driving the animals before them. Others are out of sight but not out of sound, banshee wails carrying across the countryside, the frightened animals fleeing before them. The avalanche of flesh on the hoof descends into the center of an ever tightening spiral.

Many canyons join together before entering into the narrow chasm of steep sheer cliffs which form Red Tank Draw. The whole village is coming together here, banging drums, striking sticks, clapping hands, and screaming; the circle closing shut. The animals run before this terrible onslaught of humanity, rushing towards the narrow chasm of stone, the canyons channeling together into this one slender passage. Antelope and deer jostle shoulders as they dart between boulders. Hidden in ambush strong men wait for the animals to enter the trap. Javelinas snort and snuffle in a tight pack. Jackrabbits dart and weave. The men string up nets, pulling them tight from one side to the other, preventing escape, entangling legs and hooves. Men with clubs dart into the fray, wielding savage blows and quick death.

A herd of elk enter the narrow canyon, the bellowing of the giant beasts filling the red rock gorge. Men atop the cliffs drop small boulders hoping to crush skulls. Some elk fight back; kick and bite, head butt and trample, the huge brutes bursting past the frail barriers of net cords and human beings. Some elk escape, maybe a deer here and there. A jackrabbit scampers just beneath a sandal and lives another day. Other animals are not so fortunate.

As soon as the bloodbath ends, the people break down into specialized work units. Old, young, women, men, all have assigned tasks. Meat must be butchered. Hides have to be skinned with sharp precise stone knives and then tanned. Children stretch tendons into cords. Bones are harvested for tools. These communal hunts are so important in building a tribal identity. Imagine small dispersed bands of people harvesting wild grasses, flowers and seeds, enjoying the bountiful harvest of spring in small family units when the place of stars in the sky signal for folks to gather. These cooperative hunts provide fresh meat, material wealth for the home, material wealth for trade. Afterwards the villagers exchange gossip and commerce. They celebrate with dancing, gambling, and flirting.

Perhaps.

Petroglyph interpretation is always a slippery slope. No one knows for certain how to interpret individual petroglyph symbols, let alone entire panels. Even Native American elders frequently disagree about the message which is being conveyed by pieces of rock art.

So perhaps not.

But perhaps so and if it is, I like to think that after enjoying their carnivore feast the people would gather at the petroglyph site, where the red rock cliffs are still close enough together to make the voices echo. No drums are needed in such a tight space, the clapping of hands is brisk and sharp. The pounding of the dancers feet provides a steady beat. Did voices rise in Sinaguan song of celebratory praise at this very place a thousand years ago? I always imagine the voices of the people rising as one as they thank the herd of petroglyph animals migrating across the mythic landscape. They sing the praises of the shaman in the antlered headdress, the high priest copulating with the spirit of the deer, a ceremony meant to ensure that the bountiful herds of game animals will return next spring; again and again. And again.

Deer were once human creatures who died and came back as higher beings. It is not easy being people, the burden of language is tremendous. Language puts strange thoughts in your head. It is easy being a deer. Their lives are beautiful and graceful. The deer voluntarily return each spring, these creatures who were once human and who are now higher beings. The deer return to celebrate Venus's dance across the sky, willingly sacrificing themselves as food so that we may stay alive forever. The people gather where the narrow cliffs of red rock come together, clapping hands to the beat, stomping their feet in dance. The people celebrate by singing the words of a song whose lyrics have been carved into stone for centuries and centuries.

Antelope Ghosts

I was in Mexico, on the edge of the Gran Deseierto when fourteen antelope went racing across the desert plains. The antelope were faster than the truck as the poor truck tried to traverse the bumpy bumpy road. These were Sonoran pronghorns a slightly smaller subspecies than what lives on the rest of the continent but from what I could tell they were every bit as swift. Antelope can fly, running a mile in a little more than two minutes. Back in the Ice Age there was a prehistoric cheetah who used to run around North America and that is why the antelopes had to be so fast. The cheetahs went extinct thousands of years ago but the antelope are still fast.

The Gran Desierto antelope, all fourteen of them run together, leaping sagebrush and the bizarre multitheaded barrell cactus which hug the ground there. The tiny antelope are so fast and all turn so sharply, not quite in unison, some of them stumbling. They run just a few steps in the new direction before they turn again and double back in their original direction. Our small caravan of trucks rumbles across the desert, dust kicking up as we leave the antelope behind us. We are headed towards Crater Elegante, an ancient extinct volcano whose crater stretches two miles across. Once the Crater Elegante weather gauge went seven years without rain. This part of Mexico is among the driest deserts in the world. The tall steep mountains to the west block off the rain. The earth is parched here. Volcanic cinder cones dot the landscape. Sand dunes drift here and there, piling up wherever the wind pushes them. Twisted stone, black and red lava flows,

117

frozen in mid wave, look like craggy coral reefs, and stretch across the sandy landscape for miles and miles. The Native Americans who lived in this sparse, harsh landscape, the Hia C'ed O'odham, had a reputation as sorcerers.

This is the home of the Sonoran pronghorn. Fourteen members of this rare subspecies run alongside the truck. A few days later I return home to the Unites States and read the newspaper. I am surprised by a headline which declares that the Sonoran pronghorn is in danger of going extinct. There may be only five hundred or six hundred Sonoran pronghorn left in the world and I have just seen fourteen of them running together. I still remember the very first time I ever saw a Sonoran pronghorn.

I was driving along a bumpy dirt road (as if there was any other kind) in the Cabeza Prieta Wilderness, just barely on the Arizona side of the Mexican border, when a future ghost suddenly burst across the road. It was an antelope who suddenly exploded from the grass, ran alongside my truck for several strides before turning sharply into the desert, disappearing in a flash. The small population of Sonoran pronghorns is divided evenly between The Gran Desierto of Sonora, Mexico and the Cabeza Prieta Wilderness Refuge and Bombing Range. The government conducted a scientific study to determine if the military exercises being conducted on the bombing range were harming the shy swift herbivores. What they discovered in this driest of deserts is that the bomb craters left behind by the military exercises tend to collect rainwater and that these miniature ponds in the middle of this brutal desert give the antelope more waterholes and make them less susceptible to ambush predators.

This nearly extinct species of antelope, this future ghost, bursts from the grass and races along side the truck. A stand of tall grass is a lush place in the desert and I know this spot where the antelope emerges is a prehistoric Hohokam charco. The Hohokam were a farming culture amidst all this cactus. They were led by a cult of astronomer priests who migrated up from Mexico. The specialty of these astronomer priests was the building of canals to harvest rainwater. The ground here is littered with brightly painted pottery shards a thousand years old or more. More recently, until about the middle of the 20th century, an old shaman brujo named Jose Juan used to live here. According to reports he was a hundred and twenty years old or more. They say that Jose Juan was the very last wizard who was able to bring the blessed rain, armed only with a bighorn sheep skull, some wine, and a song.

This dry dry desert is famous for its graves. The 49ers sometimes used it as a dangerous shortcut to the gold fields of California. Sometimes they died of thirst along the side of the road, broken wagons and lonely graves lining the path. The conquistadors named this road the Camino Diablo or Devils Highway. A variety of ancient archeological artifacts cover the ground, pottery shards and projectile points, representing the O'odham, Salado, Hohokam, Cochise and Clovis cultures going all the way back to the mammoth hunters.

Unfortunately none of this archeological stuff can be carbon dated accurately because there is so much background radiation that they get dates from the far distant future. Most people suspect that our own government was using the bombing range to test low yield nuclear bombs during the 1950s and 1960s. Which our military denies, claiming it is fallout from tests conducted by the evil Soviets. I have another theory, believing that the ancient Hohokam possessed time travel technology bringing these ancient future artifacts here to warn us of the environmental apocalypse which awaits us. A rare Sonoran pronghorn races alongside me, a subspecies which my grandchildren will never see, a future ghost blessed with lightning speed, as my truck rolls and bumps over the road, internal combustion gasoline engine chugging along, clouds of dust rising up behind.

The Tree of Bees

One day after work I was walking some of the trails in the hills just west of Sedona. I go there often after work, the tourists cling to the red rocks like insects around a hive. These trails through the rolling hills gradually drop into the valley and all you can see is scrub woodlands, deer, bobcats, and the occasional raccoon. There are enough trails so I can wander every which way and do all sorts of loops to vary it up. I just have to correctly remember which trailhead holds my car. I was walking along on a beautiful afternoon that was drifting lazily towards twilight when I passed by a juniper tree. As I passed by the juniper tree I heard a tremendous buzzing sound. I said to myself as I walked by "that tree must be covered with flowers". Then suddenly I stopped dead in my tracks. It was a juniper tree and they don't have very big flowers. Besides this tree wasn't even blooming. I saw a split in the tree trunk and the gap in the wood was crawling with bees. I had stumbled upon the hive. That summer I hiked out to the hive many times and took many wonderful photographs, all of which looked more or less the same. It was probably more pictures than I should have taken. A few times I agitated the bees with my camera and in particular the flash. Some of the bees took off from the wood buzzing angrily around me. I ran down the trail, screaming like a sissy girl.

I decided to discover if I could find the tree of bees under the full moon. It was much easier than I thought. In the daytime most of the bees are out flying and doing the things that busy bees do but at night all the bees return to the hive. The buzzing was loud and incredible. Not only were all the bees inside the tree at night but they were all flapping their wings rapidly. With all the bees stuffed inside the hollow of the tree, the inside of that tree must have

been extremely hot. The bees were all working their wings in synchronicity creating air conditioning on a warm summer midnight.

Ants

According to David Attenborough insects were the first creatures to emerge from the sea to the land. After billions of years they are still the most numerous creatures on the earth. It is believed that the total weight of insects outweighs all the other species of the world combined. When one thinks of how many beetles it takes to outweigh one whale or a komodo dragon that is an outrageous number. It is believed that the ants all by themselves outweigh all the people. When people try to tell me that human beings are the highest on the food chain I just laugh. What about the ants? I for one welcome our insect overlords.

Gary Every

Entryway

I saw something most peculiar today.
an anthill whose hole
was surrounded by countless
tiny lavender flower petals.
It was a lovely doorway,
a lavender entrance,
tiny and mysterious
and who knows how far it goes.
One can imagine a labyrinth of tiny tunnels
just beneath the surface of the earth
but who knows for sure
unless you could shrink down
into miniature size
and see for yourself with your own tiny eyes.
What would you see
once you had gotten past the flower petals
and tiny green leaves.
Would you enter the Antosphere,
the empire beneath the earth
where ancient queens rule with autocratic authority.
Would you feel the trembling of the soil
beneath a summer thunder shower,
or would you learn to love
the melodic rhythmic rumblings
of deep fault line cracks
far beneath the earth.
Living inside the planet,
instead of on the surface
can you feel the gentle pulls of gravity
from astronomical events,
tugs of the tides of the moon,
comets passing through.
That tiny ant hole, a miniature door
surrounded by tiny lavender flowers
just might be the entryway
to wherever you need to go.

Peridot Mesa

Standing atop Peridot Mesa
on the Apache reservation
beneath a sky of cerulean blue,
so fragile and pure
as if I could punch a hole through the clouds
if I sought divine intervention
for crisis earthly or spiritual.
On the horizon the mountains shimmer,
a deeper, darker hue
than blue or purple could ever hold,
whispering secrets of granite metamorphic mysteries.

The mesa's crown provides a view
better than any throne
free to prophets, fools, and mystic wanderers.
The ground is littered green crystalline,
layer upon layer of gemstones,
jewel encrusted volcanic rocks,
as if some helicopter bombed the hilltop
with glittering broken green glass.

And the ants crawl across the earth,
tiny insects picking their path
between jeweled fragments,
wandering among mazes of green crystals,
tiny inhabitants of Oz, the Emerald City.
I tower above them,
vistas stretching before me,
imagining myself a wonderful, wonderful wizard.
"Damn!" I say, slapping at my pant leg,
one of the ants is biting the king.

Gary Every

Ant Altar

In the jungles of El Salvador
the people make offerings to obscure Mayan gods,
gifts of incense, corn, and gold
and upon stone altars where blood once flowed,
blood pours once more.

The archaeologists have filed the proper papers
to excavate the ancient city
and try to discover lost wisdom.
The local Mayan peasants don't care
what the government agencies in the capital say.
This altar is theirs
and when the archaeologists refuse to scare
the peasants come armed with farm tools
and blood pours once more.

Still the elders say the gods are angry.
The fire ants scurry across the jungle floor,
stashing seeds in their holes.
A sure omen the elders say
of rain in six weeks.
The mountains tremble, soil ripped apart by earthquake,
and the wet slopes avalanche with mud slides
leaving the guilty nowhere to hide.
The elders say only the ants will survive.

A tiny ant carries a seed twice his size
up to the stone altar
where the peasants make offerings
to obscure nearly forgotten gods.
The ant leaves his seed
amidst the local gifts of incense, corn, and gold
and walks away
all six of his feet
stained with sacrificial blood.

Rose Canyon Bear

There was one summer when we were young when my brother and I got a job working together building custom homes in the foothills. It was hard work but a pretty good job. We got the job through David's friend Andy Seal. His father Larry Seal owned the construction company. Not that we ever called him Larry - it was always Mr. Seal. He was a big strong stern man with a gentle sense of humor. If work started at six oclock in the morning then we were at the job site at 530 unloading the truck, unwrapping wires, and getting things ready so that when six o'clock rolled around we were ready to work fast and work hard.

As a young man, Mr. Seal had worked summers building Rose Canyon Dam on Mount Lemmon. It must have been hard work gathering and moving the large heavy stones which make that dam. Back in those days manual labor was much cheaper than machines but it was the type of hard work which builds strong backs and muscular arms. Mr. Seal used his strong right arm to earn a spot on the college baseball team as a right fielder and relief pitcher. Being on the baseball team helped pay for his engineering degree but Mr. Seal couldn't deal with being behind a desk all day and eventually returned to making things with his hands, driving to work in the dark and unwinding electrical cords at first light.

I was thinking about Mr. Seal that morning when I was hanging out on the dam at Rose Canyon Lake at first light, walking along those stone walls and certain they would hold my weight, hold back those floodwaters, because I knew of the work ethic of the man who built them. It was strange how I had ended up at the dam at sunrise. There was a Baja Music Festival up at the ski lodge on top of the mountain and all the campgrounds were inhabited by rockers, punk rockers, and folkies. It was a weekend festival and there was a big bonfire party Saturday night. Unfortunately the party got out of hand and before you knew it LSD and fireworks were being passed around. To me that was a bad combination, LSD, and fireworks, the beginning of some tragic story that ends "And that's how I became known as eight fingered Gary." So I went back to my tent and went to sleep. I was chided for being such a nerd but to this day I still got all my fingers. Whether I still got all my marbles well that is a subjective opinion.

So there I was at sunrise, standing atop the dam. Rose Canyon Lake was silent and beautiful, the fading colors of the sunrise still reflected atop the surface of the placid waters. There were two fisherman on different points along the shore. I walked along the water's edge, enjoying the crisp cool of the morning. Then I saw her - the cinnamon bear.

She came strolling out from behind the trees her considerable flesh and muscles rolling beneath her bright red fur. She was the prettiest bear I have ever seen. The cinnamon bear was a little smaller than most bears and she must have been young, still wearing a puppy face. Her coat was so so red for a black bear. The red red fur was thick and luxurious, I just wanted to cuddle like she was the world's biggest teddy bear, rubbing my face in all that plush hair.

As the bear approached, the closest fisherman to her bent down to gather up his supplies, fishing poles, tackle, bait, and jacket. The bear suddenly charged, rushing halfway towards the fisherman, stomping her bear feet and woofing. In a flash, the fisherman dropped all his gear and ran into the forest like he was an Olympic sprinter. You are absolutely not supposed to run when confronted by a large wild animal, allegedly it triggers the predator and prey response, but the bear did not care. The beautiful cinnamon bear strolled over to the fisherman's discarded

things and began to eat his bait. Then she devoured his lunch in great gulps, paper bag and all. The cinnamon bear worked her way around the shore in no particular hurry, turning over rocks and stones, eating bugs, grubs, crawfish and large spiders.

Gradually she approached the other fisherman. He looked a little nervous. I was a little nervous too. I was standing right beside him. I walked away from the shore and scrambled up the stone dam, hand over hand. The fisherman was still looking nervous but I was feeling better, about fifteen feet in the air. Something about the feeling of all that stone beneath my feet, left me feeling secure.

The bear charged the second fisherman. He had quite a bit more gear than the first guy, the tackle box was bigger, there were buckets of different types of bait, he had a lawn chair and an umbrella for later when the sun came out. The red bear stopped halfway, stomped her feet and woofed. The fisherman turned to face the bear and shouted obscenities at the lumbering bruin. The bear took a couple steps forward and the fisherman grabbed his umbrella, pointing it forward like a spear as if he was prepared to joust that bear. The cinnamon bear stopped, reared up on her hind legs and pondered, shaking her head from side to side. Then suddenly the cinnamon bear roared, dropped to all fours and rushed towards the fisherman with fangs flashing. The fisherman leapt into the lake. It was cold water, really cold water, but the fisherman didn't seem to mind.

The bear stepped forward, slapping her front paws into the water, splashing the water high above her head. The fisherman swam on the edge of the deep water, moving gracelessly with kicking legs and flailing arms. The bear turned her back on the swimming fisherman and began to eat his bait. The fisherman thrashed through the lake like a wounded seal and about thirty feet down the shore he scrambled back on to land and ran into the forest. The bear didn't care. She was busy devouring his bait buckets. I opened my camera.

The cinnamon bear was so beautiful. Her red fur glowed in the reflection of the camera lens. The cinnamon bear's long long tongue writhed serpentine and prehensile, slurping and smiling. Click. Click. Click. The photographs were amazing, she was so beautiful. I fell in love with the cinnamon bear. I could be happy the rest of my life with the cinnamon bear. Click. Click. Click. Click. My camera shutter kept opening and closing, capturing beautiful images of a happy happy bear in a red red pelt.

Then the flash went off. This annoyed the bear. She stood up on her hind legs and tilted her head to the side, looking perplexed. It was a great shot so I took it again. Flash. Click. The cinnamon bear was extremely annoyed. She walked to the end of the dam, to the stone stairs. The bear placed her two front paws on the stairs. I walked away towards the middle of the dam. The bear returned to her breakfast, plowing through salmon eggs and canned corn. I crept back to the edge of the dam and focused my lens on a close up. I got a great picture of the bear's face. She was roaring. The bear rushed to the edge of the stone stairs. I hustled away. The bear turned around and I immediately started back towards my photographer's position. Instantly, the bear wheeled around and began to climb the stairs.

Gary Every

Don't Panic! I told myself. Yet there was nothing more that I wanted to do than panic. Instead, I pretended I was calm and turned around, walking away from the bear. The cinnamon bear placed her front paws on the dam and then her back paws. As soon as those back paws climbed onto that sturdily built dam, I could feel the stones groan beneath the muscle and bulk. I walked a little further into the middle of the dam. The bear followed. I stepped a little quicker. The bear quickened. The dam did not feel as comforting and safe as it had before. I did not have to look back to see the bear following me, I could feel her footsteps shuddering the concrete and stone, rattling the dam which held back all that lake water. I was almost to the end of the dam where I could dismount. I was about thirty feet above the ground on one side and a few feet above the deepest part of the lake on the other, walking a narrow cap of concrete. I could feel the cinnamon bear coming nearer, closing the gap between us. Anxious to get off the dam, I lengthened my stride. The bear loped forward, powerful legs bounding. The cinnamon bear grunted as she ran, two...three...four, giant steps as the dam shuddered beneath her. The front paws pounded the concrete like thunder and the bear's nostrils exploded with every burst of exhale pelting the back of my head with bear snot. I was experiencing fear on a deep genetic level, the absolute terror of being prey. With every bear step the dam trembled like a minor earthquake, like there were cracks rippling through the stone, as if the dam were about to burst and all the waters of Rose Canyon Lake were about to go rushing down the steep rugged mountain slope, rushing waters carrying flotsam, jetsam, boulders, bones, and trees, flooding the city far below in a wave of turbulence. Me and that bear floating down those steep granite canyons, riding the white wall of water like demented surfers.

I panicked. I leapt from the dam, falling to the earth from about twenty five feet high, hitting the ground hard with an "ooof" before rolling down hill.

The bear stopped chasing me, went back and ate her lunch. I stopped taking her picture and the bear left me alone. Besides, my camera was broken.

Gary Every

Bear Dance

My friend Jerry lives in a teepee,
hidden amidst the oak covered hills.
He points to a shallow mountain pass
and says, "Last storm, I was playing my drum to the rain
when I could swear that I saw
a bear silhouetted on the ridge."
As we ramble between the cholla and the scrub brush,
he says, "I was a little afraid,
so I played my drum loudly
to frighten him away."
We climb to the mountain pass
and discover where a tall tree
has been struck by lightning;
a branch is split and splintered,
the bark is charred.
Beneath the tree
is a pile of bear shit;
several piles.
Some of the scat is fresh;
with bits of paper inside -
trash bear.
This mountain pass is apparently a corridor,
a regular bruin highway
to the edge of our rural suburbia.
I tell Jerry,
"You had better beat the drum loudly,
to scare the bears away."
He shakes his head.
"It will never work.
Bears love to dance."

Hackey Sack Orcas

The ferry boat pulled out of the harbor from Prince Rupert Canada so gently that I did not notice. My Molson Ale never spilled from where it sat on the table. It is impossible to drive to Juneau Alaska, one must arrive either by boat or air. If one wants to take a car then the ferry boats are the answer and you can start all the way down in Los Angeles or even San Diego One can begin the journey further north in San Francisco, Seattle, or Vancouver. I began in Prince Rupert, British Columbia driving through miles and miles of beautiful wet western Canada to get to the tiny port town.

The boat left from the Prince Rupert harbor and started chugging slowly north up the Alaskan Channel. The only reason the shore was there at all was because the mountains shot up right out of the sea. There was shore on either side, islands and earth rising steeply upwards with thick groves of North American rain forest trees. The black dorsal fins of killer whales poked up from the water as small pods of Orcas swam the frigid seas. Bald eagles perched on craggy rocks or atop dead tree snags.

I could only afford accommodations for the car so for thirty nine hours on the boat I just had to figure out how to stay alive without a room. It wasn't hard, there were restaraunts where one could buy food and I discovered one deck that had tanning beds, so that as you floated past the rain forest and occasional glacier you could prevent your skin from getting too pasty and pale. I pulled two or three of the tanning light chairs together, turned them up full blast and was able to catch a decent nap underneath them that got me through the night. Feeling refreshed in the morning and after a good hearty breakfast I climbed to the top deck where I joined an impromptu hackey sack game. My soccer skills came in handy and I was able to help keep the little cloth ball afloat with my new friends and comrades. Every now and then someone would make an overzealous kick and the hackey sack would sail high into the air. So high that I almost expected one of the eagles to drop from the sky and snatch it mid air with a fierce greedy talon. Instead the sack would arc high into the air, sail just beyond the edge of our deck, and then plummet to the floor of a deck below. One of us would scamper down the stairs and race along the deck below looking for the fugitive sack. Usually that person would return via a different set of stairs and the hackey sack would be tossed aloft once more, bodies contorting and writhing, giggles filling the air.

Someone began to film us playing hackey sack as if we were natives conducting some sort of bizarre dancing ceremony. We mugged for the camera, people performing their showiest spins and kicks. Naturally, many of these kicks went awry and we spent a lot more time running up and down the stairs fetching the sack. When we got off the boat in Juneau one player offered to do laundry for all the hackey sackers. While carrying our bundle of dirty clothes down the street he asked a pretty girl where was the closest Laundromat and she invited all of us to a party. She called up her friends and they roamed the streets of Juneau gathering more tourists for the party. That was my introduction to Juneau. In no time at all I was using my out of state fishing license to snag salmon and gathering all the raspberries, blackberries, gooseberries, and salmon berries that I could eat. It felt like going completely native, waiting for the arrival of the solstice when the drums would beat and we could perform the hackey sack dance, singing songs in praise of Orcas.

One of my all time favorite hikes began with a hearty breakfast at the Hungry Bear Café. The Hungry Bear didn't have individual tables but rather long wooden picnic tables with benches that ran all the way across the resatarunt, communal style dining. As I was conversing with my neighbors, a beautiful young Native American woman, sat down with her two children in tow. She told us stories about hitchhiking across Alaska and how sometimes she would be dropped off in the middle of nowhere and sometimes wait for days until someone picked her up. Sometimes bears would come to visit while she was waiting. This Sacagewea siren told us bear stories all morning long until at last with my belly full of breakfast, I paid my bill, threw on my backpack and hiked down to the end of the sidewalk where the trailhead to climb Mt. Roberts was located.

Mt. Roberts is the highest mountain in Juneau but Juneau starts at seal level so it really isn't all that high in elevation even if the climb is rather steep. Mt. Roberts was one of the most beautiful hikes I have ever taken. The incredibly steep mountain ridges held plenty of slopes filled with talus and scree. Where the mountain did hold soil it was incredibly green. Sometimes it was so green that the thick foliage filled the earth with so much shadow that it became black. As the trail slowly wound up the massive granite spire I got a better and better view of picturesque

Gary Every

Juneau. First I could look down to the wooden sidewalks and Victorian buildings, including the Hungry Bear Cafe. As I climbed higher I could see more of the city, some of the wider more modern streets, filled with traffic, trucks and fast food chains on every corner. Huffing and puffing as I gained in elevation I could look down on the harbor, seeing the rows of docked boats. There were ships coming in and out of port and as I climbed I could watch the seafaring vessels traveling up and down the narrow channel stretching north and south, navigating between the tiny islands.

It would have been perfect if it weren't for the whistle pigs. Whistle pigs are more formally known as marmots. They are sort of like rotund tailless beavers and yet they are somehow able to whistle at ear splitting frequencies for extended periods of time. There you are hiking above the alpine and walking into a beautiful flower filled meadow, overcome with sunshine and beauty, and suddenly a rather fat rodent stands atop his burrow and whistles sharply to let all the other fat rodents know there is an intruder coming. Even John Muir had a dislike for marmots. Listen there goes another whistle pig, shrieking at an ear splitting frequency for an extended period of time. The marmot gulps a deep breath and then whistles again. Sort of makes you cheer for the eagles.

I did my best to ignore the whistle pigs and slowly trudge onwards and upwards. Climbing higher I looked down on the airport where a number of airplanes were coming and going, buzzing through the air like giant mechanical insects. From my high vantage point I was looking down on the airplanes and they looked so tiny. The airplanes and occasional helicopter were going in every direction. Some flew above the channel, some followed the coast line and others climbed above the mountain walls soaring out over the open ocean. As I kept climbing, gasping for breath, I eventually attained the peak where for the first time I could look down upon the chain of mountains rising up out of the sea. The island mountains kept rising and rising out of the water, chains of islands stretching three or four deep, jagged rock slicing through the waves and shooting upwards towards the sky. It was not until I had reached the peak of Mt. Roberts that I could look out beyond the last mountain jutting out of the sea to view the flat expanse of water which stretched all the way across the biggest ocean in the world, eventually crashing into Japan, thousand of miles away. Then turning and looking to the east, in the opposite direction, the mountain ranges stretched higher and higher until at last the bald craggy granite heads were replaced by snowcapped peaks. The snow capped peaks kept climbing until you could see hundreds of miles into neighboring British Columbia where a startling peak called The Devil's Paw rises to over 14,000 feet. From the ocean to 14,000 feet, what a view. I could not help myself, there atop Mt. Roberts, inspired by the overwhelming beauty of the world, I began to perform the non native Alaskan summer hackey sack Orca dance, feeling on top of the world.

Gary Every

Western Tanagers

Grandma Purtymun filled Oak Creek Canyon
from wall to wall with Himalayan berries
sprawling thick vines, white flowers
and red berries which turn black and juicy
but our town is not named after her.
Instead it is named after our first Postmistress
a gal named Sedona Schnebly
who was famous for her apple pies,
apple pies which were such a delight
they could have made George Washington tell a lie.
We hike through the remnants of the apple orchards
which are adorned with western tanagers
hundreds of little yellow birds
with orange bellies and red heads
which float from tree to tree
like fluttering avian jewels.
Their brightly colored orchard adornment
stops all hikers dead in their tracks.
So happy I laugh,
speaking with an old friend I just met
our toes in the frigid stream waters
discussing great American literature
Mark Twain, Thoreau,
Hemingway, Abbey, and more,
words echoing off the canyon walls like anthems.
Imagine giant spectacular chunks of mountain
adorned with tiny beautiful brightly colored birds
which flit here and there, then here again.

Juggling

On the outskirts of Las Vegas, flames leapt out from under the hood. The alternator was on fire. Flames jumped up a good two feet from the crevice where the hood lay against the frame. Robert and I were on our way to Yosemite where a freak summer snowstorm had dumped twelve feet of snow on the high mountains. First we had Las Vegas. We had a plan for counting cards that we were certain would make us money playing blackjack, enough to pay for the backpacking trip and bring home a profit beside. It was no problem buying an unexpected car part along the way.

We swapped out the alternator in the parking lot of the parts store and drove to the nearest casino. Our blackjack system failed miserably and we lost almost all our money at Circus Circus. We had just enough cash left for lunch and not quite enough for gas but we would worry about that on the way home. We ate lunch, watching the trapeze artists, eagerly anticipating Yosemite, when we saw the most amazing thing.

There was this old guy wearing a flannel shirt, suspenders, and a flattop crew cut haircut. The old guy approached one of the Circus Circus clowns and whispered something in his ear. Next thing you know the clown handed over his balls - all three of them. The guy in the suspenders began to juggle while the clown stood there and watched. Turned out the old guy was on vacation from Ringling Brothers and his wife had always wanted to see Vegas. While the old ordinary guy juggled, his little old lady wife stood behind him, beehive hairdo towering high, and one by one more and more clowns arrived, watching in amazement. More clowns gathered around to watch until fourteen brightly colored clowns stood around the juggler, clowns with big shoes, oversized bow ties, red noses and frizzy green hair, watching every move of the most conservatively dressed man in Las Vegas with awe and wonder.

Hiking the high country in Yosemite, Robert and I got lost almost immediately. Snow markers on the trail are eight feet high, and the freak summer snow storm left twelve foot high drifts, so we got lost almost immediately. The hills were covered with a smooth pristine blanket of white, the trees rose up in white covered clumps and the granite mountains rose high above us, little wisps of cloud clinging to the peaks like the last gasps of a bald man's hair. We had no idea where the trail was but it is hard to feel lost when you are surrounded by so much beauty and splendor.

I knew I would like Tom as soon as I saw him. In the middle of all that snow, he was just as lost as we were. One look into his eyes and I could tell Tom was surrounded by beauty and splendor too. Plus, standing knee deep in the snow, he was hiking in shorts. Since we were all lost anyway we decided to hike together. Tom had hitchhiked all the way out to California from Massachussets. He had a unique gimmick for catching rides. Tom would stand by the side of the road and juggle. When cars came by he would juggle with one hand and stick out a thumb on the other hand. Worked like a charm.

We set up camp beside a roaring waterfall. There was a weasel living in the rock pile beside the tent. The long slender mammal was wearing his ermine white coat and we couldn't stop him from raiding our camp as he slithered in and out of rock crevices. Still it was fun chasing him, Tom, Robert, and I encircling the small hill of rocks, the weasel using his long slender body to wiggle in and out of tunnels. We would catch a glimpse of the weasel coming out at one spot, all three of us descending with a great deal of whooping and hollering. Before the weasels tail had completely exited one tunnel, the head was already entering the next doorway. He would slither away only to pop out somewhere else. The weasel hung out around our campsite all night long, darting out from the shadows on the edge of the campfire to steal fallen dinner scraps, scampering away with his looted treasure, escaping deep inside the labyrinth of tunnels crisscrossing the small hill of rocks.

That night Tom began to juggle. Once in a while he dropped a ball. Tom told me it was important to drop the ball sometimes. He said he could blow through every trick he knew in about four minutes and it tended to leave people completely unimpressed - looked too easy. The idea was to start slowly, even drop the ball once in awhile, and then slowly build up to the harder tricks, ball over the shoulder, ball under the leg, take a bite from the apple, juggle four balls and so on until the tricks looked hard. Tom began to tell me the true story of the John F. Kennedy assassination, juggling the whole time. He explained how LBJ and Richard Nixon were in on it together and then Tom threw a ball over his shoulder. The conspiracy was tied to the rise of the Dallas Cowboys and the decline of the Boston Celtics. Tom replaced one of the juggling balls with an apple, lunged forward in mid circle and took a bite from the apple, still juggling. William Randolph Hearst, the inspiration for Citizen Kane himself, was somehow involved in this conspiracy assasination theory but I can't remember exactly how because by that time Tom was juggling four balls at once. Suddenly he rifled a ball forward, the ball ricocheted off my forehead and returned to his palm, rejoining the circling rotation without interruption. There in the Yosemite high country, mountains covered in snow, protected from the cold only by a roaring campfire, thieving weasel hanging out on the edge of camp, Tom entertained me with one of the most amazing performance pieces I have ever seen.

We sat around the campfire, drinking hot chocolate. Tom taught Robert how to juggle. Eventually the clouds began to slowly cover the stars. This was bad. If it snowed again, no matter how slight, we might not be able to find our way out. Tom pointed out that as long as we all remembered which way we had hiked in, there was no problem. There in the darkness surrounding the campfire, we all pointed in the direction we thought would take us back to where the car was parked. Like foolish characters in a Three Stooges movie we all pointed in different directions.

We awoke early in the morning and I discovered that during the night the weasel had climbed a tree, slithered out along a branch, and dropped down a rope to raid my backpack. Even for a thief that was pretty impressive. My backpack was filled with apples, granola, pears, and oatmeal, but the only thing the weasel ate was my toothpaste. He consumed nearly an entire tube of toothpaste. We ate a small breakfast, broke down camp and followed our footprints for two days until we got back to the car. Robert gave Tom a lift to the next trailhead and we started home.

This all happened shortly after I turned eighteen and to this day it was one of the most incredible backpacking trips I have ever taken. I learned that you can be surrounded by beauty and splendor and yet still be lost but it is not all that bad. I learned that sometimes the biggest clown in the room looks the most ordinary. I learned that life is nothing if not a juggling act, especially politics and history. Sometimes those ideas which stick with us are not the best ideas but those presented with the best showmanship. It does not hurt to drop the ball once in a while just to capture people's attention. Most importantly, of all the woodland creatures who live in the forest, weasels have the prettiest teeth.

Gary Every

Peregrine Falcons

These small swift flacons hunt other birds. Climbing high in the sky, they fold their wings and drop down on the prey from above, capturing it in mid-flight. Peregrine falcons are believed to be the fastest animals on the planet. I remember climbing the highest peak in Big Bend National Monument as a big storm was approaching. I heard a bird screeching. I looked out beyond the mountain to the open sky, where I found myself looking down on a peregrine falcon, the fastest creature on the planet.

Big Bend Adventure

A peregrine falcon soars
within a stone's throw of our skulls.
Tim and I climb up the pines
towards Emory Peak, the highest vertical twist
in Big Bend National Park
as the storm rolls in, the thunder booms,
and the clouds obscure
the Chisos Mountain cliffs.
Rain slickens the rock
as we climb the peak's pinnacle
to touch the lightning rod
as proof of our adventure
between ourselves and God.
The storm screams lightning
and somewhere in the drifting misty fog
the peregrine shrieks;
the echoes careening off cliff and canyon wall
like maniacal laughter.
Tim and I release the lightning rod
before racing the storm and the darkness
down the trail
with great big smiles on our faces.

Magic Bats

My friend Jerry, has undertaken the shaman's path. We huff and puff as we hike uphill, bathing in glorious moonlight. Our moon shadows march along beside us much sleeker and more graceful than our real selves. The trail winds along the ridge top, naked and exposed to the heavens. A soft warm wind climbs the mountain and thEN suDDENLY!!!

There is the mad flutter of wings; a rush of a tiny swift wind, a small bat rises barely cresting Jerry's bald head before the wings spread in a glide, shadow descending into the valley.

"I knew I was special" Jerry explained, "When I realized that every time I hike during the full moon; the bats fly close enough to bless me."

FLUTTER!

Another bat hovers just above Jerry's hairless skull.

The bats have never done this to me so maybe my friend really is special. While I ponder these thoughts I notice that Jerry also wears a halo of moths. Tiny fuzzy flying insects following his path as he climbs the mountain upwards like ascending a granite stairway to the stars.

FLUTTER!

Another bat rises, glides, and descends. We continue to hike beneath the brilliant glare of the moon.

"I hope you brought some moon screen," I tease.

Jerry chuckles.

Still, if it is possible to get moon burn, Jerry is a likely candidate. The moon reflects from his chrome dome till his head almost glows and then suddenly I realize that the moths must be attracted to the light of his reflective skull. The bats arrive to feast upon the moths.

FLUTTER! and another bat with outspread wings surfs the moonlit breeze, a wind laden with a pollen scented spring.

Jerry smiles big believing he is special.

Hiking beneath the glorious moonlight, accompanied by a good friend, I feel pretty special too. Magic bats indeed!

Elk Statues

Two old men wander in the sculpture garden, a little lost amidst this tourist trap of galleries, restaurants, and stores filled with expensive knick knacks. The old men walk silently and slowly side by side. Both men wear work boots, denim pants, flannel shirts, and baseball caps. Gradually they wind their way through the rose bushes and Buddhas to end up at the life sized metal elk. They stop to reach out reverently and touch the life sized statue, bronze bovine beast raising his head proudly as if to whistle and bugle, magnificent rack of antlers with spikes pointing to the heavens like the stars of a celestial constellation.

Elk are large and magnificent beasts, so large and so stout. Highways where elk live are adorned with an abundance of elk crossing signs. You do not want to hit an elk with a car. Your car will be totaled and you may be seriously injured or even killed. The elk may be able to walk away from the collision. There are elk involved with human traffic fatalities every year. In the forests along the Mogollon Rim there are electronic signs connected to motion detectors to warn motorists when elk are near the edge of the road.

I was camped at place called Gabaldon, outside Greer the highest campground in elevation in the White Mountains of Arizona and I awoke just before sunrise. Everyone inside the tent was snoring so I snuck out for an early morning walk. I strolled past the beaver dam and tiny pond beside the campground. The light was just beginning to creep out of the corners of the sky but the sun was still hidden behind the mountains. There was fog everywhere. The mountains were shrouded in clouds. It really didn't matter that I couldn't see where I was going - I was just out for a morning stroll.

I found myself walking through a thick patch of forest, wisps of fog blowing softly in and out of trees, creating an eerie ghostlike effect. A soft cool breeze raised goose bumps on my flesh but when the wind gusted it pushed the fog away, except for a few thin strands of mist that clung to the tops of the pine trees. The sun started to peek above the mountains and for the first time I could see clearly where I was. I was in the middle of an elk herd. There were hundreds of elk scattered between the trees. In the darkness, shadow and mist I had not noticed the hundreds of sleeping brown torsos. Some elk slept on their sides and other elk cows were kneeling as they slept. Now that I was looking they were everywhere, scattered between the trees in little clumps of three or four. On the dark edge of twilight and with the fog, I had assumed they were boulders but they weren't, they were elk, hundreds of elk. Elk sleeping on their sides, elk kneeling, and even calves. Hundreds of elk and I appeared to be more or less in the center of the herd. Apparently elk don't snore when they sleep because if they did I would have heard them.

Now that they were beginning to awaken the elk snuffled and snorted. First the elk shook their heads as if trying to displace cobwebs and then they wiggled their ears. Sometimes a tongue would dart out and wrap itself from snout to eye, cleaning herself. A few cows stretched their necks and shoulders while I watched these intimate morning rituals in amazement. The middle of the herd was an impossible place to be and to this day I am not certain exactly how it happened. As the herd awoke most of them seemed blissfully unaware of my presence. One elk, with a sleeping calf curled against her side, stared at me in wild eyed disbelief. As I walked closer her eyes filled with panic and her shoulders twitched. Her long legs began to unfold as if she was preparing to rise abruptly. I realized for the first time what a position of danger I was in. If my presence in the middle of the forest was suddenly detected and I was considered a dangerous predator then the herd would stampede and I would be trampled to death.

I angled my path slightly, giving nervous mama a wider path. Her sudden movements had awakened her baby, who twisted his neck and wanted to feed. With her child suckling the mother elk remained calm and motionless. She watched me continuously as I tiptoed softly and slowly through the rest of the herd. One elk stood up and startled, running away, nearly causing two or three others to do the same. I braced for the stampede but I only had another step to get beyond the last tree and step back into the meadow with the beaver dam and gurgling creek. Then the elk lay back down.

Those are the memories I am thinking about while the two old men wind their way slowly through the sculpture garden as if they are making a pilgrimage to the life sized elk statue. Almost as if they cannot really believe they are doing such a thing they reach out haltingly to touch the giant bronze beast. The old men stretch their fingers, expecting fur instead of metal. They touch the life sized elk statue, look at each other and smile, expressing themselves with wordless nods. Perhaps the silence has been practiced, hours of quiet waiting for the ambush. Maybe everything there is to say, every joke, every story, every insight has been said before, during countless conversations over thousands of campfires. Perhaps the most important things will never be said. How our time on this earth is finite. How every breath is measured. How every heart beat no matter how wild and excited or calm and serene moves us one step closer to that inevitable ending.

Then there is the elk. There is the bond between the men and the elk. There is the bond between the two men as they work to together to chase the elk. Is there any need to mention how the pursuit of an animal so magnificent becomes a religious quest eventually. The old men smile and nod silently. There is no need for words because surely somewhere in the forest a beautiful brute of a bovine beast calls with a tremendous bugle - fur, hoof, antler, and bone quivering with the song of the mountain as it echoes from stone to stone.

Red Squirrels

One of the biggest environmental controversies in Arizona involved the building of telescopes atop Mt. Graham in the 1980's. This controversy drew media attention from around the world. One of the proposed telescopes was sponsored by the Vatican and it became easy to draw battle lines composed of heroes and villains, with the pope opposing the Apache who held the peak sacred, a repeat of the colonial wars when conquistadors rampaged over the Native Americans and through this land in pursuit of God, gold, and glory. Eddy Vedder of Pearl Jam came to speak at a rally in Phoenix whose audience numbered in the thousands.

The first legal obstacle to the building of the Mt. Graham telescopes was the red squirrel. The red squirrel is native to the Pinaleno Mountains but with the introduction of the much larger, more aggressive kaibab squirrel, who most likely hitched rides aboard logging trucks to reach the Pinalenos, the habitat for the red squirrels shrank until they lived only on the top of the mountains, exactly where the telescopes were proposed being built. The University of Arizona, the leaders in the construction project were accused of trying to rush through building before the proper environmental impact studies were undertaken. When completed, the environmental impact statement determined that the presence of the astronomers and more importantly the trash they would occasionally leave behind would provide an important food source for the red squirrels. The red squirrels had been forced to the mountaintop because the resources were too marginal

Gary Every

there to support a kaibab squirrel population. Far from harming the red squirrels the building of the telescopes and in particular the astronomer's trash would probably be an asset.

At that point in my life I was a student at the University of Arizona and felt inspired to write a letter to the editor of the student newspaper The Arizona Daily Wildcat. The letter proposed that since everyone seemed so concerned with the health of the red squirrel population, and since kaibab squirrels seemed to be the problem, that we pay a bounty of 50 cents a pelt for kaibab squirell fur. So that nothing would be wasted I suggested the squirrel pelts could be sold on the U of A mall with proceeds to benefit the university astronomy club and the squirrel meat could be donated to a local homeless shelter.

At this point in my career I have been published thousands of times yet nothing I have ever written has drawn as visceral and immediate a response as that one paragraph letter. Many people were offended that I offered the squirrel meat to the shelter, feeling that I was degrading the homeless, although I personally have found squirrel stew to be rather tasty. Some people are offended by the thought of anyone wearing fur. Others are completely anti-hunting and all I can do is respect their right to disagree. Wherever I went on campus people mentioned the letter. I suppose its only appropriate - I have always been regarded as a little squirrelly.

Herons and Cranes

Banjo Burch and I were fishing at Picacho Lake/ Coolidge Marsh. We had brought along his sailboard but the sail wasn't really doing us any good because the reservoir was far more marsh than lake, dotted with trees, reeds, and bushes. It was far too difficult to try and capture the wind and still maneuver between the clumps of trees. We were able to navigate by kneeling atop the narrow sailboard and paddling, cruising atop the small stretches of flat open water and turning sharply between the clumps of trees. The fishing wasn't bad, a few small bass and catfish dangling from the ends of our fishing lines. After awhile I asked Banjo to drop me off on the edge of the shore.

From there I resolved to hike around, circumnavigating Picacho Lake/ Coolidge Marsh while Banjo continued to fish. The lake was ringed with reeds and trees and had receded slightly so that I found myself hiking through a vast mesquite bosque although there were plenty of other trees mixed in such as tamarisk and cottonwood. It was a weird eerie place to be, dried moss clinging to the ground where the water used to stand. Every now and then I had to change my route slightly when the earth got too wet, my shoes sinking in the muck and mud. As I got deeper inside the vast forest of soggy trees I started to notice bundles of sticks in the uppermost branches of the tallest trees. Birds, big birds were nesting here. As I looked around I noticed more and more nests. My eyes searched the ground hungrily, hunting for fallen feathers. I wandered further and further into the heart of the soggy forest, surrounded by old and ancient trees, some of whom had three or four nests nestled at the junctions of different branches, homes hidden in the foliage. The ground was getting increasingly moist. More and more I found myself wading through ankle deep water. The water was cold. My shoes, socks, and the bottoms of my trousers were soaking wet. I began to shiver and goose bumps raised on the flesh of both arms. I sneezed.

AAAAA-CHOOOOO!

That single sneeze set off a roar you cannot imagine. All around me in the trees the wings of giant birds began to unfold. Tall and gangly birds stood up hastily in their nests, causing a shower of sticks, twigs, leaves and feathers to flutter to earth. Many of the birds cried with the harsh honking sounds peculiar to their species but all of them, all of the thousands of the treetop citizens of the soggy forest took flight, wings flapping in fast long strokes as they launched into the sky. The sound was incredible, honking and squawking everywhere. So many birds flapping at once that the motion of the wings pushing air made a ruffling sound like a muffled roar. All these giant birds flapping their giant wings, all of them lifting into the sky at once, generated a wind which blew across my face and rippled the shallow waters.

There were hundreds of birds spiraling upwards, a long column of herons and cranes spinning higher and higher into the wind, clouds, the sun and maybe beyond. Not only was I startled by the incredible number of birds who launched into the sky but there was an incredible variety of birds, great blue herons, white cattle egrets, green backed herons, comorants, black crowned night herons, and the tall angular frames of sand hill cranes, a bird which stands over four feet tall. There were hundreds and hundreds, perhaps even thousands of birds flying above me, climbing and climbing their spiral staircase to wherever it is angels fly. Many Native American cultures believe that a sacred feather can help carry one's prayers into heavens like wings of love. If that is true then that afternoon, with those thousands of birds circling above my head, each and every feather carrying a different prayer, then that explains why I have been so blessed.

Gary Every

 I circumvented the lake and caught up to my friend Banjo at sunset just as he was pulling his boat out of the water. The fishing gods had been good to Banjo. He had pulled lots bass and a couple catfish out of the water. On the ride home we spoke excitedly of whom we would invite to the fish fry. During the drive Banjo looked over at me and said "When I saw all those birds in the air I just knew that you were in the middle of it."

 Indeed I was.

Breeze Rider

I think my favorite summer
was when Banjo Burch bought the sailboard.
The shape of a sail
when it catches full wind, taut,
with just a little flutter along the edge,
is designed to mimic the shape
of a bird wing.
I'll never forget sailing on moonless nights
when the sailboard moved effortlessly,
like I could tilt the mast
and point us upwards,
sailing out amongst the stars
until I reached mythical kingdoms
like Atlantis, Oz, and the
Seven Cities of Cibola.
All those stars reflected
on the surface of the water,
peering into my own image,
motion blurring myself
into a shimmering illusion,
tiny wake following behind the sailboard,
the footprints of my path,
quickly buried beneath the waves.

Gary Every

Great Horned Owls

I hike often under the full moon and sometimes when I do I am fortunate to be greeted by the "who who whooo" of a great horned owl. These birds are large, over two feet tall and with wingspans which stretch several feet. When one frightens a great horned owl from its perch the big bird's natural response is to lift off and fly right towards your head. This defensive mechanism works pretty well. As soon as the heavy birds leap into the air, beak extended, talons out and giant wings flapping furiously towards your head your natural reaction will be to duck. As soon as you cower the owl will fly low over your head and beyond, escaping easily.

The one thing that will not happen during such an event is that you will not hear the sound of the wings flapping. Owls are nocturnal hunters and hunt more by sound than eyesight. As a result, owl feathers are aerodynamically silent in flight. If you find a feather in the forest and are not certain whether it belongs to an owl or hawk, wave it up and down next to your ear as if it were flapping. If you fail to hear the sound of the breeze then it is most likely an owl feather. For this reason the owl kachina of the southwest is usually depicted holding a bow and arrows, owl feathers on the end of each shaft. Great horned owls have an incredible sense of hearing but almost no sense of smell. Perhaps this is why great horned owls are the only natural predator of skunks.

I mentioned that when I hike at night under full moons sometimes I am greeted by hooting owls. Sometimes but not always. Great horned owls are migratory creatures, making annual loops within a region, stopping and harvesting different food sources as they become available. For instance every year the great horned owls roost at the University of Arizona. You might think that wise old owls spending time at the local university is only appropriate and indeed it was a wise move on the owls part. The owls appear every year near the end of spring, almost the beginning of summer break. Sometimes the presence of the owls causes unexpected problems. In the 1980's there were owls perching near the entrance to the main library on a regular basis. During final exams the library saw a steady flow of students coming and going. Often times the owls would be startled and take flight, launching themselves at the students heads. The frightened students

Gary Every

would flail and stumble as papers, notebooks, pens and papers flew in the air. Sometimes the students were Native American and in many native cultures owls are considered extremely bad omens. So bad that sometimes the Native Americans were frightened from entering the library that day. At the Native American's request, the owls were eventually scared off with hoses and loud noises, moving to different parts of campus that did not see quite as much traffic.

The owls had arrived at this institute of higher learning with a purpose. Every year when the spring semester ends, many university students realize that the cute little puppy or kitten they adopted and raised throughout the school year now has nowhere to live when the student must leave for the summer. Often times the prodigal student is warmly welcomed back at their parents home but Fido or Fluffy is not. Many of these young defenseless pets are callously left behind in alleyways and parks. The owls return annually, always the same time of the year, and feast.

Saguaro Raven

If saguaros have memories, and some of these cacti giants are centuries and centuries old, do they remember the years past when the harvest of saguaro fruit was celebrated with songs, ceremony and dance as the beginning of the new year? A blood red wine was made from the cactus fruit and the people would sing to the frogs, magicians of transformation, begging them for blessings. Lightning splits the sky as if the clouds are erupting with thorns and then the watery blessings fall to earth. The people smile, harvesting a treasure like plucking the jeweled ruby eye of Quetzacoatl.

This day, in this modern world, from my car, I spy a giant green cactus alongside the highway with a black as midnight raven on top. His iridescent black black feathers absorb and reflect the desert heat. Even as my car goes whizzing past, the raven maintains fierce eye contact, staring directly inside me. I pull over the car and glare back. This raven is not easily intimidated but he is easily bored. He goes back about his business, bows his head and buries his black beak inside the pale white blooms, causing the flower petals to dance and writhe. I am perplexed, ravens are not usually listed among the pollinators of saguaros.

From my car parked alongside the edge of the road, windows rolled up and air conditioner on to escape the blistering desert heat, I watch the raven atop the saguaro. He hops from the crown to the top of an arm, long slender green cactus arm holding saguaro flowers like a bashful bachelor offering a beautiful bouquet. The raven rustles his black feathers before burying his head inside another blossom. The bird tilts back his head, opening and closing his beak, gulping something down his throat. Then I realize, these saguaro blossoms, smelling faintly like cantaloupe are filled with bees. As the large thick bill probes and penetrates, rustling petals and stamens, the raven is searching for bees, interrupting their floral sex. The worker bees are busy collecting their treasures of golden pollen but before they can return to the hive they are gulped whole and devoured.

The raven feasts upon bees, digging amongst the cantaloupe smelling flowers for unwary pollinators. The large thick black bill probe, raven gulping another winged insect whole. He tilts back his head, working dinner down his gullet. With his head buried in the blossoms, it causes the white flower petals to writhe and dance.

The wind tosses raven from his perch, black wings flapping above the pale desert landscape. He wears a golden pollen crown upon his nose and beak, an unintended consequence of this feast of bees. The raven flies away while the saguaro soldiers of this cactus army, continue their march down the ridge, multiple arms raised in threatening gestures as they attempt to recapture the cities, reclaiming ancient lands. This invasion will take centuries, perhaps millennia but they are saguaros and they have the time and most importantly they have the patience. The wind gusts again and raven caws, calling as he ascends the steep slope. The breeze is gusting so hard that as it blows across the cactus needles it makes a high pitched whistling song, almost as if the saguaros are singing.

Breath of Iiyotoi Birds

The sacred mountain of the Tohonno O'odham is named Baboquivari, which translates as mountain which is "fat in the middle". It is a magnificent mountain. It shoots right up out of the earth in towering spires. The earth is extremely flat here except for the mountain. It is a landscape one of my old geology bosses would have described as "tuna can flat". Stand on a tuna fish can and you can see forever. Then that magnificent mountain shoots up out of the earth, fat in the middle before tapering off to a tall bald peak, granite fist poking into the heavens. Elder Brother Iiyotoi sits atop Baboquivari Peak and watches events unfold, occasionally meddling in the affairs of men.

The flat landscape spreading out in all directions has almost no trees, but there are saguaros everywhere. The giant green cactus tower above the landscape, green heads poking above all else, many arms reaching skywards. Some of these saguaros are fifty and sixty feet tall. Some may be centuries old. When I was a child we were told that some of the giants such as Man of Many Arms may have predated Columbus. In recent years, the estimated age of saguaros have been revised considerably downwards. It takes about sixty years before a saguaro sprouts a first arm. They are a little taller than a human then. You see some saguaros towering dozens of feet high and with eight, nine, ten or twelve arms and you wonder how much history they have lived through.

There is a species of insect called the vinagaroon which lives on saguaros. Vinagaroons are bad ass looking bugs who should probably be the inspiration for some terrible monster in a way cool science fiction movie. They are related to scorpions, and although painful and irritating their sting is not as dangerous as a scorpion's. They are more thickly armored with much heavier pincers than a scorpion. They are black and ugly, scuttling across the desert like crabs. Some vinagaroons spend their entire lifetimes on a single saguaro. It conjures the image of an intelligent society of vinagaroons gathering together to speculate whether it might be possible that other saguaros hold life, possibly even other intelligent societies of vinagaroons, and if so is intercactii travel possible?

The Tohonno O'odham begin their calendar year with the harvest of ripe red saguaro fruit in early July. The ceremonies and songs associated with the saguaro fruit harvest are intended to bring the summer monsoon rain storms. According to O'odham traditions, if the rains do not come, the desert will grow hotter and hotter until it bursts into flames, the earth burning into ash in a flaming ball of spontaneous combustion. The saguaros play their part, the tall green cactus reaching into the sky, straining and stretching their long green arms towards the clouds. The clouds float aimlessly by while the desperate cacti reach as high as they can. Finally one green arm reaches higher than it has ever reached before, just barely touching the bottom of a cloud. The saguaro thorns puncture the cloud, just like popping a balloon, and the rains begin to fall.

Some saguaros have multiple arms and in those instances when the arms branching off the main trunk are close together, sometimes the junction of arm and trunk hold bundles of sticks. These large bundles of sticks are bird's nests, usually raptors, sometimes owls. Driving out to the base of Baboquivari Peak, through the forest of countless saguaros, it is amazing how many large bird's nests are scattered across the terrain. Many of the nests hold fuzzy chicks. In this dry thorny landscape large predators like mountain lion or bear are rare. There is no large game here but there is plenty of smaller animals, jackrabbits, cottontails, rats, mice, ground squirrels, lizards, and a wide variety of snakes. The numerous types of large hunting birds who live here, hawk, falcon, golden eagle, and crested caracara are top of the food chain.

The Tohonno O'odham reservation is vast and wide, about the size of Connecticut and yet less than 10,000 people live there. My car rolls across the flat desert landscape for hours while the sea of saguaros expands in all directions. We drive through the tiny town of Sells and turn south towards the Mexican border. As we drive past the local grocery store there is a large mural painted on the wall. Against a black background the mountain which is fat in the middle is depicted with the full moon rising behind. Off to the right is a starscape with planets including Saturn. To the left of the sacred peak there is a mythological Native figure wrapped in a blanket with a feather in his hair. This mythological figure is blowing his breath outwards, creating a cosmic wind which stirs the universe - the breath of liyotoi.

We drive south, almost to the international border and then take a left at Topawa, the sprawling metropolis of mighty mighty Topawa. Topawa consists of a handful of reservation style government houses, a few mobile homes and some stray dogs roaming in different directions. A crested cacracara feasts on road kill, fuzzy feathered head and thick bill tearing flesh from the carcass on the asphalt. From there the road is dirt for many many miles. Our vehicle rolls through the forest of countless saguaros, bundles of sticks clutched closed to their green thorny bosom by the upraised gently curving arms. From inside the bundles of sticks big eyed chicks stare in wonder as we drive along the flat wide dirt road, clouds of dust rising up behind. We navigate this ocean of giant cactus making a direct beeline for Baboquivari Peak on the horizon where the sacred mountain erupts from the earth. Does Elder Brother liyotoi sit atop the peak and watch our gradual approach? Just as we reach the foothills of Baboquivari and the trailhead which marks the beginning of the ascent we turn away from the mountain, journeying a much less traveled path. In the heart of the vast saguaro sea there is a large stone outcropping which arises from the desert sands in a single blob. This blob of stone is about fifteen feet high and fifty feet long and on one side it is covered with petroglyphs and pictographs.

Some of this rock art is nearly a thousand years old and some of it is much much older. The oldest stuff is painted on to the stone and reminds me of the Gallery Beings in Utah, other figures consist of abstract looping lines which mimic the shape of the mountain. Some images are faint and others bold. Most of the rock art is white but some icons, especially the older ones are red or yellow. There are hundreds of images clumped together on one side of the stone, stars, mountains, stick figure men and abstract geometric designs. Modern prayer offerings are left at the base of this ancient shrine. These prayer offerings include lottery tickets and bullets. Other prayer offerings are much more moving such as the tiny American flags left in honor of O'odham soldiers serving overseas in the United States military. There are always teddy bears along the base of this petroglyph wall. When I have inspected the bears I have found that they are sitting on intricately painted pottery shards and there are photographs of little children taped to the undersides of the bears. The children depicted in the photographs are being prayed for by whomever left the teddy bears.

WHOOOSH!

A red tailed hawk flies to the stone wall and then shoots upward, coming close enough above our heads that we can hear his wings flap. The hawk rises swiftly into the sky, folding up his wings so they catch the breeze and he sails across the saguaro sea.

It is a powerful place to stand, this small outcropping of stone amidst this flat flat piece of earth, sacred mountain rising on the horizon. The wind rushes across the desert, hot blasts of whirlwind rattle the creosote as they race above the sand. I stand before this wall of petroglyphs and stare in wonder while the wind bursts with gusts which promise the salvation of summer monsoons arriving soon.

WHOOSH!

A pair of Coopers Hawks leapfrog above the stone outcropping and into the sky. I debate whether it is sacrilege but end up removing my camera from my backpack and take photographs of the petroglyphs.

Whoosh! Whoosh! Whoosh!

Three vultures rise up one after another, each using the stone outcropping as a leaping point into the sky. The wind rushes forward across this flat landscape, picking up momentum the whole time until the gusts of breeze burst into this stone outcropping in the middle of the flat landscape and are pushed abruptly upwards. The wind must rise straight up here, the birds catch it under their wings and fly directly up like riding an elevator. This obscure clump of rock in the middle of nowhere is covered with ancient petroglyphs and modern prayer offerings, and I think maybe that is because here the prayers are gathered

Gary Every

by the birds and then the birds are lifted into the heavens
by the breath of liyotoi.

Sparrows

Weary after work, I pause at home just long enough
to change shoes and hit the trail.
My roommate thinks I am crazy
to commit acts of strenuous exercise.
My hiking boots stride along the earth
while the heavens spot with storm clouds and lightning,
and rain falls on the far horizon.
The sporadic nature of the approaching weather
leaves some mountains illuminated
and other mountains in shadow.
The sun strikes an oblique angle
setting slowly, hanging low in the sky,
colors filling the clouds;
warning of the disappearing day and the onset of nightfall.
My footsteps pound the trail
startling chickadees and sparrows
from the scraggly bushes where they roost.
Seventy, eighty, maybe a hundred tiny birds
all fly into the air at once
in a frenzied flurry of flapping wings and feather.
There is a story in the Koran about Jesus as a young boy,
standing alongside a riverbank
and fashioning sparrows out of clay.
An elder chastised young Jesus
for working on the Sabbath
and the petulant messiah responded
by turning the clay vessels into real birds;
setting them free on the breeze
with a flurry of feathers and wings.
Today the tips of the branches still quiver
from the sparrows launching into the heavens
soaring every which way across the colors of the sunset.
My roommate wonders why I hike
after a long days work
as I receive a hundred tiny blessings.

Gary Every

Wings

I like to run across the desert,
my feet leaping high above the earth,
holding a feather in each hand,
gripping tightly, holding them out at arms length,
stretching, stretching, expanding the tips of my wingspan.
Today, I fly with owl feathers
found beneath the arms of a saguaro,
bird's nest cuddled to the green bosom in fond embrace.
Other times the feathers I discover
belong to a dove or cactus wren,
and once, on the first day of spring,
when the sun hung low in the sky,
flush red with the promise of summer,
I found two cardinal feathers
tangled among a tower of cholla thorns.

I run and run and run;
air circulating, legs thrusting, heart pumping.
I am a rumbling, thundering, hydraulic machine,
stumbling across the earth at a rapid pace;
flying.
You can't get hurt if you don't land
and you'll never crash
if you don't fall down.
So the trick is to glide forever,
like a soaring hawk;
know you're cool.
My heels dig deep into the dirt
scattering frightened deer from the underbrush.
The breeze tugs on my feathers, pulling, pulling
but I will never loosen my grip
for these are the wings of my soul.

Javalina Pumpkins

I was working as a chef at a high priced health resort. We made low fat gourmet foods and part of teaching people how to lose weight was giving classes in cooking and nutrition. In the demonstration kitchen we would teach classes on things the resort guests could prepare at home. For the October holidays, it was my responsibility to make decorations and carve pumpkins. Carving pumpkins was not a culinary art I was particularly skilled in but it paid overtime hours and I was willing to give it a shot. For inspiration I tried to picture the face of each of the seven dwarves; Doc, Sneezy, Sleazy, Wheezy, Bumpy, Dumpy, and Lumpy. When I was done I took a step back to check out my handiwork and realized that I had made reasonable replicas of the tortured grimaces of my over worked, under paid, stressed out co-workers.

The guests were pleased with my pumpkin artistry and I received several nice compliments. The next day revealed how quick and fleeting was the fickle finger of fame. The dishwasher took down all my decorations and the seven grinning ghoulish gourds were banished outside the demo kitchen door where Housekeeping was supposed to properly dispose of the pumpkins. Except the people in Housekeeping never quite got around to it. That night when the guests began to arrive for class the pumpkins were still lined up outside the door, grinning inanely and starting to smell just a little bit.

I think it was that slight tang of pumpkin odor which attracted the javelinas from the edge of the desert. While the guests were in class and listening to the lecture, dining on what they considered to be gourmet food; the javelinas were in the outdoor hallway, dining on the pumpkins, which probably is considered gourmet dining in the world of wild beasts.

When the class ended and the guests tried to leave the classroom, the door swung open and hit one of the baby javelinas on the butt. The tiny hairy javalina squealed. Some of the guests squealed too. A pair of the more aggressive guests tried to swing the door open just wide enough to squeeze through and politely pass by the pumpkin dining javalina. In doing so, they accidentally cut off the two babies from the rest of the herd.

The mother javelina went wild, squealing and honking in the way that only feral beasts can. The guests were taken aback and hesitated. The male boar showed no such uncertainty. He snorted and stomped his hooves. He huffed and puffed and with steam bursting from his nostrils he charged the door. The guests were barely able to sneak back inside and close the door before the weight of the large male boar crashed against it with a shudder, his tusks digging deep grooves into the wood. The mother javelinas rushed over to comfort their babies. The boar stomped his hooves triumphantly.

The guests waited a polite interval and tried the door again, assuming that the javelinas would be done with their business. The javelinas had other ideas. Seven pumpkins is a lot of food and the desert beasts were enjoying their meal leisurely. Besides, as near as the male boar could tell - he had the upper hand. Every time the door would open the slightest crack the male javelina would snort, stamp his hooves, lower his tusks ready to charge, and the door would suddenly slam back closed; frightened tourists behind it. The javelinas would return to their jack o' lantern dinners.

Gary Every

Eventually security was called and I am sure that was quite a sight. Those guys come through the kitchen looking for food during their many coffee breaks and I am certain that they were more frightened of the javalinas than the javelinas were of them. Eventually the javelinas finished their Halloween meal and retreated back into the desert of their own volition.

Desert Riparian

Only an Arizonan
would think of a flat stretch of sand
as possessing an up and down stream;
a flow of soil
holding the scavenged treasures
of high tide monsoon flash floods -
rivers stones, pottery shards, and old coins.
Today, on a hot summer day,
the sandy surface of the arroyo
is dry as a bone
causing the flowers to wither;
dieing slowly from thirst.
Only the trees remain;
thorny mesquite,
glittering golden leafed cottonwood,
the fragile lavender flowers of desert willow,
and the deep thick sprawling roots of walnut trees.
Two black winged butterflies
land on the sand,
drinking thirstily from the hidden pieces of moisture
buried between the grains of soil.
The wind gusts,
causing the two winged lovers
to somersault through the sky
and rustling the leaves of the trees
like a gentle shaking of dreams;
sounding like a soft stream trickling across rocks.
The cooling breeze races along the ribbon of trees
creating a waterfall of leaves
while the wind whispers of wetness.

Gary Every

Butterfly Bath

I drag my fat old man ass
out on the trail
to try and do some running.
As I proceed into later middle age
and do battle with my growing midriff
I am forced to run slowly
and then forced to stop entirely on the uphill.
I catch my breath
at a spot where the arroyo takes a deep bend
and the sand is dark and moist.
Here the butterflies come to drink,
tiny wings beating like floating flowers
they alight to drink water from the damp soil.
I go and stand amongst these hovering insects.
They flutter and bob beside me,
orange and black above my shoulder,
yellow and blue behind my knee
and a small cluster of white and yellow butterflies
hovering just beyond my belly button.
The soft silken powdered wings mist my flesh
with brightly colored butterfly dust
The fervently beating wings create a breeze
which washes over me softly
like bathing in colors.

Get Your Ass To The Pass

Something about the brutal blazing heat of Nevada, just outside of Death Valley, makes you want to do nothing more than lay in the shade and watch the sun do all the work as it travels across the sky. Doing geology work in Nevada I learned a healthy respect for vultures. The winged creatures were visible wherever you went across the vast landscape, black and white appearing here and there in the sky. The vultures float effortlessly, patiently riding thermal updrafts like a slowly winding spiral staircase climbing and climbing into the clouds. Doing my geology job often entailed trudging across the desert while carrying heavy burdens of rocks, picks, shovels, and sticks. While I was drenched in sweat and groaning from my labors it seemed as if the vulture's travels were much easier. As I would march and march I would gradually approach the vultures getting close enough to see them adjust a few wing feathers slightly and notice how their flight patterns immediately changed, circles expanding or closing depending on the conditions. After the vulture deemed he had reached a high enough elevation he would fold up his wings and soar across the landscape, suddenly traversing the earth swiftly.

Once I saw a small flock of vultures on the edge of a forest fire. Intense heat from the roaring blaze created incredible thermal updrafts and the vultures were acrobatic in a way that I have never seen them before or since. They swooped and soared, dove and rolled, hanging sharp banked turns. The vultures took advantage of the extreme circumstances and floated on the winds of scorched earth like skateboarding punk rockers, performing trick after trick, surfing the winds of apocalypse.

The Mint 400 rolls through this part of Navada. The Mint 400 is an off road automobile race from Las Vegas to Reno. Dune buggies, beat up SUVs, jeeps, hummers, trucks, sand rails, and over powered station wagons race recklessly across these desert sands and deep arroyos. I was working geology on Bare Mountain, clinging to those steep slopes when I saw a giant cloud of dust forming on the horizon. The dust was soon followed by the infernal roar of internal combustion engines. The dust cloud grew larger and larger as it approached. It kept approaching, gradually creeping closer and closer and as it did I realized how far away it was and just how big the cloud of dust was. Dust stretched from horizon to horizon and rose hundreds of feet in the air in a big ball of earth and wind. I was working high on the mountain clinging to a steep slope as the automobiles raced beneath me, quickly rolling past. Noise everywhere, so loud it shook the slope I was clinging to. Then the reckless offroad racers were gone. Silence everywhere. It was one of the most absurd things I have ever seen. Soon enough the roar of their engines disappeared but the cloud of dust hovered for days, growing a little smaller all the time until it disappeared bit by bit.

One of the benefits of working a job in Nevada is you often get to see wild mustangs, sometimes every day. Not outside Death Valley, the landscape outside Death Valley is too sparse to hold mustangs. It is the only part of Nevada where you do not see mustangs. What you get on Bare Mountain is wild burros, descendants of the burros who used to roam these hills following prospectors. Generations of wild burros have been wandering these hills for over a century.

Gary Every

Hikers who bushwhack often find themselves on game trails. Deer paths will take you to hidden waterholes but your eyes must be sharp to follow the trail. Cattle trails meander pointlessly from here to there but the big bovine brutes clear a path about cow shoulder wide and unfortunately cow shoulder high. While walking a cow trail you discover yourself ducking frequently. If a cow trail meanders pointlessly until you end up someplace stupid you have no right to complain because cattle are not a species known for their intelligence and you are dumb enough to follow them. Javalina trails are thorny, winding through scrub brush and sometimes you have to get down on your knees to pass through a javalina trail. In contrast wild burro trails are like superhighways. The burros follow each other in a tight line as their sturdy hooves compact the earth, creating a flat smooth hiking superhighway.

I remember one time Dick Ahern and I were climbing a steep slope on Bare Mountain. Dick and I just looked at each other in amazement "Whoa! Did you see that?"

It was one of those moments of unexpected illumination. Dick and I were climbing up a volcanic gorge, searching for signs of gold. It was a very steep gorge; impossibly steep; one ridge a volcanic tuff purple and the other side of the chasm was a sun bleached pink. In geological time that ridge is washing away like wet sand but that afternoon it presented quite a challenge as we huffed and puffed up that ridge. As near as I can figure, what happened was a combination of the angle of the sun, the slope of the ridge, and the ascending flight of that vulture. Just as the bird flew overhead these things combined to make the shadow of the vulture grow into a silhouette with a fifteen foot wingspan like it was a pterodactyl or baby dragon or saber toothed eagle, the shadow cloaking us entirely for an instant. Reflexively, we cowered, some primordial prey instinct kicking in.

Dick and I just looked at each other in amazement, "Whoa! Did you see that?" It was one of the most incredible things that I had ever seen and then it was over. I wiped the sweat from my brow and resumed earning my peasant wages while in the canyon far below a jackass resumed braying.

Beatty, Nevada celebrates their prospector heritage with an annual Get Your Ass to the Pass Race. A large corral is built and a number of wild burros are captured and placed inside. An equal number of racing contestants voluntarily step inside the corral. The wild burros mill about, idly wandering inside the corral wherever they wish to go. The contestants are all bunched together at the starting line, waiting for the starters whistle. The whistle blows and the Get Your Ass to the Pass race begins with a cluster of cacophony. The contestants scurry about the corral, lariats in hand. The burros become frightened and charge in different directions, some kicking, some braying. The contestants use their lassos to try and capture a burro. There are an equal number of burros and contestants but some burros are just too ornery to be catchable so contestants often find themselves competing for the same burro. Once a contestant has captured a burro they must lead the animal to the far end of the corral where they load the burro with prospector's gear, pick, shovel, bedroll, lantern, coffee pot, and gold pan. The laden burro is now led to the opposite end of the corral where the contestant builds a small fire. According to the rules the burro is allowed to help in the making of the fire but most burros are not too helpful in this regard. Once the campfire is burning the contestant quickly whips together a batch of pancake mix. A black cast iron skillet is placed on the fire and a single pancake is placed inside. First racing contestant to flip his flapjack, brown it and devour it whole, wins the race. The burro is not allowed to help with the eating of the pancake.

Most of Nevada hosts wild mustangs, the only exception is on the edge of Death Valley where the wild burros roam. Nothing inspires visions of freedom and speed like a herd of wild mustangs. Mustangs have hippy like hair, manes and tails draping off the horses bodies. When the horses run and gallop all this hair flutters in the wind. The wild horses often run, just because they can. The mustangs rise up on their hind legs kicking their fore hooves into the air, whinnying and laughing, taunting the wind.

There was one time working in Nevada we saw the same small herd of wild mustangs every day for almost a month. The herd consisted of a beautiful brown stallion with a white star on his face and three mares, two of whom had foals that never left their sides. One day a rogue male appeared on the horizon, grazing a little ways off. Over the next few weeks he attempted to steal the childless mare for his bride. It was a like a slow formalized ballet. Every day the rogue became a little more aggressive and every day the two stallions battled for position, carefully measuring their turf. They kicked up dust and whinnied. They charged and bluffed. They whinnied and rose up. Then they kicked up more dust. The next day they would meet again and be a little more aggressive, charge a little harder, whinny a little louder and kick up a bigger dust cloud. Finally after about two weeks the two stallions did battle. The whole fight was over in seconds, a couple kicks, a bite, and a whole lot of dust before the challenger ran away over the hills, his tail between his legs, never to be seen in these parts again.

The next day we were working along a ridge when the triumphant stallion and his three mares galloped into the pasture below us. I don't know if the shovels I was carrying made my silhouette look different but the stallion became suspicious. He got between me and his mares and his children, agitatedly running back and forth. He threw up clouds of dust in whinnied in my general direction. I stomped my feet on the ridge, my work boots pounding the soil like a war drum. I used the shovel to throw dust over my head, imitating the way stallions challenge each other. The mustang below the ridge, the patriarch of his herd, grew greatly upset. He rose up on his hind legs, kicking his forelegs into the sky as he snorted and cried. I used the shovel to toss dirt over my head. I stomped my boots on the earth. I threw dust in the air again. Then I let loose with my best whinny, tossing my head into the sky and crying out.

Apparently my best whinny is not good enough. As soon as he heard my horse imitation, the stallion relaxed. He no longer galloped back and forth, prepared to answer my challenge. My whinny was so weak and feeble that the stallion trotted a short distance away from me and in what I assume is the ultimate equine insult, grazed with his butt to me.

Gary Every

Mustang Dream

Vultures spiral, climbing columns of hot air,
maneuvering the invisible columns of dry air
that carry coarse grains of sand
which plaster themselves amidst the sweat and hair
plaguing my eyes.
Changes in wingspan make the vultures orbit more elliptical
as my back bends, weary from my labors as a geology mule.

Flat Nevadan valleys, receded glacial seas,
where scraggly bushes blossoms - looking trampled,
resemble the struggling spring time of an outer world moon.
The man working transit
directs me, my shovel, and bundle of sticks
towards the ridge top.
On the shimmering horizon the oasis illusion gleams,
summoning a black stallion,
four mares and a foal to graze
on the scarce grasses that rise like whitecap foam
upon the rolling waves of sandy sea.

The fierce eyed stallion stares,
nostrils flaring with snorts of indignation
that interrupt the wind itself.
White socked hooves stomp,
raising clouds of obscuring dust
which float challenges across the landscape.

I am stuck on ridge top, rod in hand,
while the transit man triangulates.
The bored horses gallop away,
racing ghosts and shadows,
ankle length hair fluttering in the breeze
like staccato flamenco guitar strings
while
I measure the earth into random rectangles

Chachalaka!

I climb the highest peak in Arizona; a staircase of volcanic basalt twisting up the spine of a ridge as rocky and bumpy as a dragons back. I stop for breath on the steep climb, pausing to photograph wildflowers. The mountains go by many names. All these separate peaks are really the remnants of one ancient super volcano whose top blew off 1.8 million years ago and changed the weather on the entire planet for years. They are known on the maps as the San Francisco Peaks because local legends claim that from the very top, on an especially clear day, you can see all the way to San Francisco. This is not true. Others claim the name came because the mountains were first placed on the map on the feast day for Saint Francis. The highest peak in the state of Arizona goes by the name Mount Humphreys, even though no one seems totally sure who Hunphreys was. The Spanish called them the Sinagua Peaks; meaning "mountains without water" because of the dry lava beds which surround them. The Native Americans refer to this snowcapped cluster as the Kachina Peaks, the Arizona Mount Olympus home to the kachina spirits; Kokapeli, the Corn Maidens, and of course Crow Mother who rules the roost.

I am alone atop the sacred peak for almost half an hour before I am joined by a man and his curly haired dog. He is a raft runner, leading tours down the Grand Canyon, following the traditions of John Wesley Powell. I share some granola. He offers me a stick of green apple gum. He says, "I chew green apple gum all day long while running the raft through the rapids in the bottom of the Grand Canyon."

Gary Every

As soon as the flavor touches my tongue I realize that it will always be a ticket to return to the top of the world. The taste of that magical gum machine will trigger memories of the Grand Canyon or maybe recall any time I have floated down a river in a raft, kayak, or canoe like Huckleberry Finn on the mighty Mississippi River, mouth full of sweetly tart sticky green saliva; heart ready for adventure.

While I am hiking down from the peak and most of the way to the car, I hear an angry squirrel screaming the forest. This does not surprise. One cannot get within a hundred miles of the mountain town of Flagstaff and not hear an angry squirrel. They are quite common. Toss a dead cat in any direction and the odds are pretty good it will hit an angry squirrel. Usually the squirrel is angry even before you hit it with the dead cat. Flagstaff is just that kind of town.

The squirrel was shouting in that teeth gnashing, angry chattering form of cursing that squirrels have perfected and some thing on the other side of the tree made one of the weirdest sounds I have ever heard.

"oo - loo - woo, oo - loo -woo, oooo - loooo - wooooo."

It was a weird sound. If you had told me that squirrel was battling a tiny extraterrestial space alien on the other side of that tree I would have totally believed you. The sound was just that weird.

"oo - loo - woo, oo - loo - woo"

I just had to run around that tree and see for myself. What I saw was not a space alien but it was almost as unexpected and strange. I ran around the tree and came face to face with the greater prairie chicken. I did not even know that Arizona had wild grouse but apparently it does. The angry squirrell ran one way and the grouse ran the other. I grabbed my camera and followed the grouse because who needs another picture of an angry squirrel in Flagstaff.

It is embarrassing to admit just how difficult it was to follow the fat flightless bird across the steep sloped forest floor. The grouse wove between logs and rocks, scurrying between the bushes so it was difficult to get a clean shot - a photo shot. While I was trying to focus and run at the same time I kicked a rock. Now I was hopping on one foot and trying keep up with a fugitive prairie chicken. The prairie chicken was winning. Turns out that the grouse family can be correctly described as fat and NEARLY flightless birds. The grouse flapped his chubby little wings as fast as he could, slowly rose up into the lower branches of one of the tallest trees in the forest. While the grouse sat there perched on his limb I shot photo after photo - nearly all of the photos turned out be a little blurry.

So the next day while I was at work in a retaraunt kitchen, I couldn't show any photographs and I ended up trying to explain to *mi cosinero compadres* in my very bad Spanish about this wild bird I had seen, a fat nearly flightless bird that was slightly bigger than a chicken and slightly smaller than a turkey, but nobody really seemed to get it. Then Manuel suddenly understood and shouted out "Chachalaka!"

I was excited to learn a new word and like I always do when I learn a new Spanish word, I wrote it down and used it in a sentence. *"Yo quieros chaka chaka con chachalaka."*

Chaka Chaka is kitchen slang and my sentence implies I want to have sex with a wild chicken. Which I do not but when you learn Spanish in a kitchen, you learn to say many crude things and not much else. Alfredo reads what I wrote and is afraid I do not understand what I am writing or else I would not be writing it. So I repeat it out loud *"Yo quieros chaka chaka con chachalaka."*

Alfredo shakes his head in disbelief. He is certain I do not understand what I am saying. He shouts *"Chachalaka!"* and tucks his thumbs under his armpits, flapping his elbows like tiny wings. He raises one knee high and clucks like a rabid rooster. It is both amazing and hilarious.

So I pretend I don't understand and ask him to do it again.

He does it again! Flapping his wings, doing his rooster walk and clucking all over the kitchen.

Turns out *chachalaka* is not a Spanish word after all. Some Mexicans had no idea what I was talking about when I said *chahcalaka*. It is a regional thing, Manuel from Morelo, Herlinda from Guerrero, Oaxaco, they all understood. *Chachalaka* is probably a Native American word whether Mayan, Zapotec, or Nahuatl I could not tell you. What I do know is that Alfredo is a big happy guy with a thick black moustache that looks like he should be on horseback in a Pancho Villa photograph. He frequently bursts into song in the middle of the workday and every time he does all the *cosineros* tuck their thumbs under their armpits and flap their wings, dancing like *chachalakas.*

Battling the Hydra

For my 50th birthday I had plans for a boating trip to a spectacular scenic lake where I hoped to disembark on the shore of a remote side canyon. After a hike that I was hoping would not be too adventurous I was expecting to discover a sixty foot waterfall with a lush desert grotto, a wet green oasis amidst a sandstone wasteland. The ancient Anasazi had written on the stone here, leaving behind petroglyphs which a guidebook described only as "exotic". The sheer cliffs which formed the waterfall held fossilized dinosaur footprints. The Anasazi would have recognized the tracks etched in stone as belonging to giant reptiles and what kind of petroglyphs would the Anasazi have drawn to commerrorate this unique place? What kind of "exotic" petroglyphs would they have carved into stone to summon dinosaur magic? What stories belonged here?

It had taken lots of research to plan the expedition. I woke up early on my 50th birthday and began loading gear into the car only to discover that the gods were angry. The highest mountain peaks in the state, the Kachina Peaks, were engulfed in thunder snow storms. The light show was horrifically majestic, lightning flashing amidst the blizzard, snow coming down in gusts of swirling white. The clouds parted just long enough for the sun to shine on a small patch of earth, snowbows hanging in the air.

Then the tornados came. Cyclone after cyclone leapt from the tops of the Kachina Peaks, where the kachinas or earth spirits live like Greek Gods atop Olympus, kachinas hurling lightning bolts through snow storms. Cyclones dropping from the mountain tops and tossing semi tractors across the highway. Rednecks in trailers picked up by tornadoes and hurled across the heavens to become beer drinking UFOS. Seventeen locomotive cars were lifted from the railroad tracks and dragged across the countryside in a giant chain. I will drive through the rain. I will hike in the rain. I will even fish in the rain but Gary don't drive through tornadoes. Birthday plans cancelled.

So there I was home alone on my 50th birthday, when I wasn't even supposed to be home at all. Feeling sorry for myself on a cold wet rainy night with a howling wind when suddenly one of the cats screamed. I was not surprised. The many cats who live in my house fight battles over hierarchy and territory all the time. Except I only heard one cat scream.

I rushed upstairs and realized something was terribly wrong because all the cats were scared. Very scared. I looked around and discovered my roommates snake had gotten out of his cage and had the littlest kitten in a vice like grip. The snake is about sixteen feet long and was wrapped around the kitten in four or five coils so that all you could see of the cat was a hind leg. The cat is named Halfway and at that point I figured that cat was about halfway down that snakes gullet. That was one big snake and that was one dead kitten. Then Halfway emitted a whimpering meow, the saddest sound I have ever heard.

I grabbed the snake and started uncoiling but the snake grabbed me as well wrapping her tail around my ankle. I unwrapped one coil from the kitten and then another. The snake hissed as I unwrapped another coil. And then I unwrapped another, until at last I could see the two heads, the one of the giant serpent and the head belonging to its intended dinner. The python twisted a middle section around my elbow as I grabbed her by the jaws, trying to force it to let go of the kitten. The snake bit harder. The kitten screamed but at least I knew it was alive. The python wrapped another coil around my midsection. I started to work my fingers under the python's jaws. The python tightened its grip on my midsection and used its tail to yank on my ankle and pull me down. Me, the kitten, and the python fell to the floor. It was at this point I began cursing at the snake and calling her foul nasty names.

I managed to stand back up and the snake uncoiled from my ankle and midsection and wrapped itself once around my knee and once around the kitten, squeezing tightly. I have to admit that I considered pulling my cell phone out of my pocket and fighting off the snake with one hand while I used my other hand to call my friend and ask him what to do. Instead I worked my fingers behind the pythons jaws and popped open his grip. The snake kept a piece of the cat's ear as a souvenir. It took both my hands to release the last coil and when I did the kitten fell to the carpet with a plop.

The kitten lay on its side, motionless.

The snake coiled its tail around the desk and used it as leverage to pull on my knee and we both fell to the floor again while the kitten lie on the carpet gasping. I was back up in a flash and using language that quite frankly is not worth repeating. I unwrapped the serpent from my torso, coil by coil, and then tried to stick all sixteen feet and ninety pounds of Bambi, (yes her name is Bambi), back into her cage. Things seemed to be going smoothly when

BAM!

In the shadow of an instant the snake had leapt off my body and attacked the kitten again. It happened so fast I couldn't even see it. I went from having a giant snake wrapping and unwrapping itself all across my torso to not having any snake touching my person at all. Bambi had wrapped herself around Halfway, five or six times. All I could see of the kitten was a few tufts of fur here and there.

So we repeated the entire process again, only faster because I was a little better at it the second time around. Uncoil, uncoil, and uncoil, and Bambi hissed again, much more loudly. I stopped for just an instant and Bambi hissed louder. I worked my finger beneath her jaws and popped them open. The kitten plopped back onto the carpet, but I could see his tiny ribs pumping back and forth. Fighting the snake with one hand, I used my other hand to lob the kitten towards the door shouting out "Run Halfway Run!"

Halfway ran, but staggering sideways as if he was badly injured. I shut the door behind him, so it was just me and the snake. This time I got Bambi back in her cage. Eventually. I walked out of the snake room, shut the door behind me and had no idea where Halfway was.

I found all the other cats first. They were all afraid. Manny (short for Manifold), the biggest cat in the house, was on top of the kitchen cabinets. In fact Manny rarely came down from the top of the kitchen cabinets for the next three weeks. He just kept staring at us all frenzy eyed like he thought we should be on top of the kitchen cabinets too. When I finally found Halfway he was downstairs in the basement hiding under the couch panting for breath. Halfway just kept panting and panting, gasping for breath, and then from time to time his eyes would roll back in his head. You could tell he was on the verge of fainting and losing consciousness. I thought Halfway had a fractured skull.

When constricting snakes get as big as Bambi they no longer kill by strangulation. They like to deal a death blow with their first strike. If all goes well, the snakes first strike will compress the chest, damaging the heart and crushing other vital organs as well as creating a great deal of internal bleeding. Strangulation only helps to bring death more quickly. Halfway kept on panting but it didn't really slow down very much by the time I fell asleep and I fell asleep not certain if the little kitten would survive the night. When I awoke in the morning, there was Halfway breathing normally. As to whether Halfway sustained a skull fracture and serious brain damage, if you knew Halfway you would understand why that was a difficult question to answer.

I would also like to take this opportunity to publicly thank Bambi for not biting my face off. If she had really wanted to come after me I would have been in serious trouble. When you consider that I ripped dinner out of her mouth just as she was nearly finished killing it, her reaction could have been much more extreme. Although she hissed, and hissed loudly, (her head is about the size of my hand) in a way that I found rather menacing, she never actually attacked me. Bambi is not poisonous but she does have teeth and she is very strong, much stronger than me. So thank you Bambi.

I will always remember my 50th birthday as the birthday when I saved a life, even if it was just a goofy little kitten. This birthday had a waterfall oasis amidst one of the driest deserts in the world, dinosaur footprints, exotic rock writings from an ancient vanished civilization, thunder and lightning blizzards, cyclones, and hand to hand combat with a giant serpent. I thought maybe such an intense experience would inspire some good poetry but I wanted to do some research first. I cracked open a book of Greek mythology and started to read about Hercules battling the

Gary Every

Hydra. That was when my roommate entered the room and asked what I was reading. When I told him he was incredulous.

"Mythology what has that got do with anything? How could mythology possibly have any relevance to your life at all?"

I just smiled and scratched Halfway atop his head, while the little kitten purred and purred, rubbing my fingers between his ears, one of which is badly scarred.

About the Author

Gary Every is the author of seven other books including Shadow of the OhshaD, which contains award winning journalism stories such as Losing Geronimo's Language and The Naichee Ceremony. He is also a four time nominee for the Rhysling Award for years best science fiction poem. His other books include Cat Canyon Secrets, Inca Butterflies, Drunken Astronomers, as well as The Saint and The Robot.

He can be reached at garyevery@gmail.com

www.ingramcontent.com/pod-product-compliance
Lightning Source LLC
Chambersburg PA
CBHW060252290526
45789CB00001B/304